WINNER'S
PLAYBOOK

ABOUT THE AUTHOR

Avery Cardoza, author of more than 15 books on beating the casino and the world's foremost publisher of games and gambling books, is America's top gambling authority. His definitive book, <u>How to Win at Gambling</u>, the encyclopedic guide to the odds and winning strategies of gambling, has been called one of the 10 best books on gambling ever written.

Avery Cardoza has counted on his gambling winnings and activities as his primary source of income for all his adult life and before. He has never held a 9-5 job.

No casino will knowingly deal cards to Cardoza, who at the age of 23, when even the biggest casinos refused him play, took his gambling winnings and wrote and published his first book, the best-selling classic, <u>Winning Casino Blackjack for the Non-Counter.</u> Today, with more than 50 gaming titles and 4,000,000 books in print, Cardoza Publishing is the undisputed leader in games and gambling information.

Though originally from New York City, where he is occasionally found, Cardoza has used his winnings to pursue a lifestyle of extensive traveling. Long sojourns to such exotic locales as Bahia in Brazil, Jerusalem, Tokyo and Southeast Asia, were followed by living stints in California, New Orleans, and of course, Las Vegas, where he did extensive research into the mathematical, emotional and psychological aspects of winning.

In 1993, Cardoza, with a partner, also started **Open Road Publishing,** publishing travel guides, and co-authored the <u>Las Vegas Guide</u>. In January 1995, Cardoza's long-awaited line of fully animated, 3-D, high resolution casino games for the computer will debut.

WINNER'S PLAYBOOK

PLAYBOOK

THE MINI-ENCYCLOPEDIA OF WINNING AT GAMBLING

Avery Cardoza

Gambling Research Institute
CARDOZA PUBLISHING

To Julian

Cardoza Publishing, publisher of Gambling Research In-stitute (GRI) books, is the foremost gaming and gambling publisher in the world with a library of more than 50 up-to-date and easy-to-read books and strategies.

These authoritative works are written by the top experts in their fields and with more than 4,500,000 books in print, represent the best-selling and most popular gaming books anywhere.

Library of Congress Catalogue Card Number 94-68041
ISBN:0-940685-53-1
Cover photos by Ron Charles

CARDOZA PUBLISHING
P.O. Box 1500, Cooper Station, New York, NY 10276
(718)743-5229

**Write for your <u>free</u> catalogue of gambling books,
advanced strategies, and computer items.**

TABLE OF CONTENTS

INTRODUCTION

You can win money at gambling, but that takes knowledge of how the games are played and the best bets to make. In this book, we're going to give you that knowledge in one quick and easy sitting, and show you how to beat the casino and be a winner.

We cover the basics of playing and winning at 10 gambling games - baccarat, blackjack, craps, lotto/lottery, keno, poker, roulette, slots, video poker - and the very exciting and tantalizing - strip poker!

We get right down to the basics here so that you'll immediately be a better and smarter gambler. And our all-important money management section shows you how to minimize losses when it's not your day, and also, how to walk away a winner when it is!

This mini-encyclopedia also includes a complete listing of the toll-free and local numbers of the Las Vegas, Atlantic City and Laughlin casinos, while the World Casino Guide shows where the gambling action is in over 75 countries and 1,000 cities!

There's also lots of fun stuff besides the meat and potatoes of winning - your own personal gambling logbook, a gambling quiz and crossword, and the wacky 52 mad, mad gambles!

There's a lot here, and all aimed at one purpose - to make you a winner at gambling!!!

WINNING BLACKJACK

You can win money at blackjack! With proper play, you can actually have the edge over the casino, and the expectation of winning every time you play.

Object of the Game

The object of blackjack is to beat the dealer. This is done by having a higher total than the dealer without exceeding 21 points or when the dealer's total exceeds 21, called **busting** (assuming the player hasn't busted first).

The Blackjack Layout

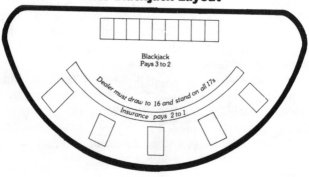

Blackjack
Pays 3 to 2

Dealer must draw to 16 and stand on all 17s

Insurance pays 2 to 1

The Basics

Casinos use one, two, four, six and sometimes as many as eight decks of cards in their blackjack games. Each deck used is a standard pack of 52 cards. While single deck blackjack offers the best odds for players, any number of decks can be beat with correct play.

Suits have no relevance; only the numerical value of the cards count. Each card is counted at face value, 2 = 2 points, 3 = 3 points, except for the ace, which can be valued at 1 or 11 points at the player's discretion, and the **picture cards** (the jack, queen and king), all of which count as 10 points each.

Entering a Game

To enter a blackjack game, sit down at any unoccupied seat at the blackjack table, and place the money you wish to gamble with near the betting box in front of you. The dealer will exchange your money for chips.

THE PLAYER'S OPTIONS

Each player gets dealt two cards, as does the dealer, and after examining them and the one exposed dealer's card, the player has several options.

He can **stand,** take no more cards; **hit** or **draw**, take an additional card or cards; **double down**, double his bet and take one more card only; **split**, take cards of equal value and split them into two separate hands; or, **surrender** - only infrequently offered - forfeit the hand along with half the bet.

A player may draw cards until he is satisfied with his total, however, once his total exceeds 21, his hand is **busted**, and he's a loser, regardless of what happens to the dealer's hand subsequently.

Drawing Cards and Standing

To *draw* a card in a single deck game, the player scrapes the felt surface of the table with his cards. In a game where both the player cards are dealt face up, the player is not supposed to touch his cards and instead scratches the felt with his fingers or points toward the cards if he desires additional cards.

To *stand* in a single deck game, the player slides his cards under his bet. In a game where the cards are dealt face up, he waves his hand palm down over his cards.

Single Deck - Hitting and Standing

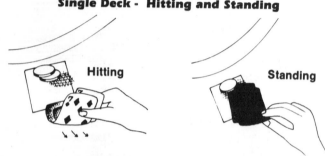

Hitting

Standing

Multiple Deck - Hitting and Standing

Hitting

Standing

The Dealer's Rules

The dealer, however, has no such options, and must play by prescribed rules. Once the players have played out their hands, it is the dealer's turn.

He turns over his hidden card for all to see, and must draw to any hand 16 or below and stand on any total 17-21. The dealer has no options and cannot deviate from these rules.

In some casinos the dealer must draw to a **soft** 17 - a total reached when the Ace is valued at 11 points.

Payoffs

The bettors play only against the dealer and must have a higher point total without exceeding 21 to win. Winning bets are paid at even money. When both hold the same total, it is a **push**, and nobody wins.

If the dealer busts, all remaining players (those who have not already busted) win and are paid out at **even money,** $1 paid for every $1 bet.

Players who get dealt a **blackjack**, an ace and any 10-value card (ten, jack, queen or king), get paid 3 to 2, unless the dealer gets a blackjack also where it is a push. If the dealer gets a blackjack, he wins only what the player has bet.

Insurance

When the dealer shows an Ace as the exposed card, the player is offered an option called **Insurance**. It is a bet that the dealer has a 10-value card underneath for a blackjack. The player is allowed to bet up to one half of his original bet, and will get paid 2 to 1 if indeed he is correct.

However, this is always a bad bet unless one is a card counter, and therefore should not be made.

WINNING STRATEGIES

Dealer Pat Hands: 7-Ace as Upcard

When the dealer shows a 7, 8, 9, 10 or Ace, hit all hard totals of 16 or less.

Dealer Stiffs: 2-6 as Upcard

When the dealer shows a 2, 3, 4, 5 or 6, cards he will frequently bust with, stand on all hard total of 12 or more. Do not bust against a dealer stiff card. Exception - Hit 12 vs. 2 or 3.

Player Totals of 11 or Less

On point totals of 11 or less, always draw (if you do not exercise a doubling or splitting option).

Player Totals of Hard 17 or More

On point totals of hard 17 or more, stand.

Doubling and Splitting

Play aggressively, taking full advantage of doubling and splitting options, as presented in the master strategy chart on the following page. (When you can double on totals of 10 and 11 only, as in Northern Nevada, hit - do not double on other doubling totals, except when holding A7, where you should stand.)

THE MASTER STRATEGY CHART

The following Master Strategy Chart gives you an extremely accurate game against the rules and variations you'll find from casino to casino. Top line represents dealer's upcard, left column is the player's hand.

For single deck games, make the plays as shown. For multiple deck games, where there is an asterisk, hit only - do not double or split.

BLACKJACK: MASTER STRATEGY CHART

Player's Hand	- Dealer's Upcard -									
	2	3	4	5	6	7	8	9	10	A
7/less	H	H	H	H	H	H	H	H	H	H
8	H	H	H	H	H	H	H	H	H	H
9	D*	D	D	D	D	H	H	H	H	H
10	D	D	D	D	D	D	D	D	H	H
11	D	D	D	D	D	D	D	D	D	D*
12	H	H	S	S	S	H	H	H	H	H
13	S	S	S	S	S	H	H	H	H	H
14	S	S	S	S	S	H	H	H	H	H
15	S	S	S	S	S	H	H	H	H	H
16	S	S	S	S	S	H	H	H	H	H
A2	H	H	D*	D	D	H	H	H	H	H
A3	H	H	D*	D	D	H	H	H	H	H
A4	H	H	D	D	D	H	H	H	H	H
A5	H	H	D	D	D	H	H	H	H	H
A6	D*	D	D	D	D	H	H	H	H	H
A7	S	D	D	D	D	S	S	H	H	H
A8	S	S	S	S	S	S	S	S	S	S
A9	S	S	S	S	S	S	S	S	S	S
22	H	spl*	spl	spl	spl	spl	H	H	H	H
33	H	H	spl	spl	spl	spl	H	H	H	H
44	H	H	H	H	H	H	H	H	H	H
55	D	D	D	D	D	D	D	D	H	H
66	spl	spl	spl	spl	spl	H	H	H	H	H
77	spl	spl	spl	spl	spl	spl	H	H	H	H
88	spl	spl	spl	spl	spl	spl	spl	spl	spl	spl
99	spl	spl	spl	spl	spl	S	spl	spl	S	S
1010	S	S	S	S	S	S	S	S	S	S
AA	spl	spl	spl	spl	spl	spl	spl	spl	spl	spl

H = Hit   S = Stand   D= Double   spl = Split

*In multiple deck games, hit only - do not double or split.

GLOSSARY

Barring a Player - The exclusion of a player from the blackjack tables when casino personnel feel a player is too skillful.

Basic Strategy - The optimal playing strategy for a particular set of rules and number of decks used, assuming the player has knowledge of only his own two cards and the dealer's upcard.

Blackjack or Natural - An original two card holding consisting of an Ace and ten-value card. Also the name of the game.

Break - see Bust.

Bust or Break - To exceed the total of 21, an automatic loser.

Card Counting - A method of keeping track of the cards already played so that knowledge of the remaining cards can be used to adjust strategies. A player that counts cards is called a card counter.

Dealer - The casino employee who deals the cards, makes the proper payoffs to winning hands and collects lost bets.

Doubling, Doubling Down - A player option to double the original bet after seeing his original two cards. If the player chooses this option, one additional card will be dealt.

Doubling after Splitting - Option offered in only some United States and international casinos whereby the player is allowed to double down after splitting a pair (according to normal doubling rules).

Draw - see Hit.

Early Surrender - A rarely found option to forfeit a hand and lose half the bet before the dealer checks for a blackjack.

Exposed Card - see Upcard.

Face Card - Also known as **Paint**. Jack, Queen or King.

First Base - Seat closest to dealer's left. The first baseman acts upon his hand first.

Flat Bet - To bet the same amount every hand.

Hard Total - A hand without an Ace or if containing an Ace, where the Ace counts as only 1 point (10, 6, A).

Head On or Head to Head - Playing alone against the dealer.

High Roller - A player that wagers big money.

Hit - The act of drawing (requesting) a card from the dealer.

Hole Card - The dealer's unexposed downcard.

House - A term to denote the Casino.

Insurance - A side bet that can be made when the dealer shows an Ace. The player wagers up to half his original bet and gets paid 2 to 1 on that bet if the dealer shows a blackjack. If the dealer does not have a blackjack, the insurance bet is lost. Play continues as usual.

Multiple Deck Game - Blackjack played with two or more decks of cards, usually referring to a 4, 6 or 8 deck game.

Natural - see Blackjack.

Pit Boss - Casino employee who supervises play at the gaming tables.

Push - A tie between the dealer and the player. Neither side wins.

Shoe - An oblong box used to hold multiple decks of cards. All 4 and 6 deck games are dealt out of a shoe.

Shuffle, Shuffling Up - The mixing of cards by a dealer prior to a fresh round of play.

Silver - $1 tokens or dollar chips.

Single Deck Game - Blackjack played from a single pack of cards.

Soft Hands, Soft Total - Hand in which the Ace counts as 11 points.

Splitting Pairs - A player option to split two cards of identical value so that two separate hands are formed. A bet equal to the original wager is placed next to the second hand.

Stand, Stand Pat - A player's decision not to draw a card.

Surrender, Late Surrender - A player option to forfeit his original hand and lose half the bet after it has been determined that the dealer does not have a blackjack. Option offered in some casinos.

Ten-Value Card - 10, Jack, Queen or King.

Third Base - Also called **Anchorman.** Position closest to dealer's right. The third baseman makes the last play before the dealer's turn.

Toke or Tip - A gratuity either given or bet for the dealer.

Unit - Bet size used as a standard of measurement.

Upcard - The dealer's face up (exposed) card.

WINNING CRAPS

Introduction
Craps is the most exciting of the casino games for the action is fast, and players catching a good roll of the dice can win lots of chips in a hurry.

The Basics
Craps is played with two standard six-sided dice, with each die numbered from 1 to 6.

Bets are placed on a craps **layout**, a large piece of green felt which is marked by the various bets possible and on which the dice are thrown.

The Come-Out Roll
The first roll of the dice is called the **come-out roll.** It marks the first roll of the **shoot** and is either an automatic winner or loser for **pass line** bettors - players betting with the dice, or **don't pass bettors** - players betting against the dice; or the roll can establish a point.

If the come-out roll is a 2, 3, 7, 11 or 12, the pass and don't pass bettors will have their bets paid or lost, and the following roll will be a new come-out roll.

Any other number thrown, a 4, 5, 6, 8, 9 or 10 becomes the **point.**

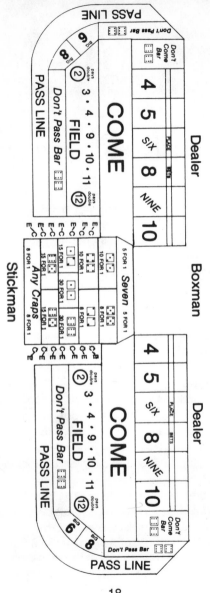

18

THE LINE BETS
Pass Line Bet
The throw of a 7 or 11 on the come-out roll is an automatic winner, while the throw of a **craps,** a 2, 3, or 12 is an automatic loser. All other throws 4, 5, 6, 8, 9, 10, become the point. Once the point is established, pass line bets win if the point repeats before a 7 is thrown and lose if the seven is thrown first. Other throws are inconsequential. Pays even money.

Don't Pass Bet
A come-out roll of a 7 or 11 is an automatic loser, a 2 or 3 an automatic winner, while the 12 (in some casinos the 2) is a push - nobody wins. Once the point is established, don't pass bets win by the seven being thrown before the point is repeated, and lose if the point is thrown first. Other throws are inconsequential. Pays even money.

COME AND DON'T COME BETS
These wagers work exactly like the line bets above except that they can be made only *after* the come-out roll, when a point is already established. (Pass and don't pass bets can be made only on a come-out roll.)

Come Bet
7 or 11 on the first throw is a winner, a 2, 3 or 12 is a loser. After, the come point must repeat before the 7 is thrown to win. Pays 1-1, even money.

Don't Come Bet
7 or 11 on the first throw is a loser, a 2 or 3, a winner and 12 is a standoff. (In some casinos 2 is the standoff and 12 is the winner.) Once the come point is

established, 7 must be thrown before the come point repeats for a winner. Pays even money.

FREE-ODDS BETS

To make a free-odds bet, the player must already have placed a pass, don't pass, come or don't come wager. Free odds bets are so named because the casino enjoys no edge on them.

Free-Odds: Pass Line

Once the point is established, the pass line bettor is allowed to make an additional wager, called a **free-odds bet**, that his point will repeat before a 7 is thrown. He may bet up to the amount wagered on the pass line and does so by placing the chips behind his pass line wager.

On come points of 4 or 10, the casino will pay 2 to 1 on a free-odds win, on points of 5 or 9, it will pay 3 to 2 and on points of 6 or 8, it will pay 6 to 5.

Free Odds: Don't Pass Line

Works the other way. Free-odds bettors wager that the 7 will be thrown before the point repeats. Since the odds favor the bettor once the point is established, there being more ways to roll a 7 than any other number, the don't pass free-odds bettor must **lay odds**, that is, put more money on the free-odds bet than he or she will win.

The allowable free-odds bet is determined by the payoff, not the original bet. The bettor is allowed to win only up to the amount bet on the don't pass line.

We'll assume a $10 don't pass bet which means the player can win only up to $10 on the free odds bet. On points of 4 or 10, the player must lay $20 to win $10; on points 5 and 9, he must lay $15; and on points 6 and 8, he must lay $12 to win that $10.

To sum the odds up, the player must give 1 to 2 odds on points of 4 and 10, 2 to 3 odds on points of 5 and 9, and 5 to 6 odds on points 6 and 8.

Don't pass free odds bets are made by placing the wager next to the don't pass wager in the don't pass box.

Free Odds: Come and Don't Come Bets

These bets work the same as the free odds on the pass (corresponds to the come bet) and don't pass line (corresponds to the don't come) except they can only be made *after* the come point is established.

The only other difference is that the free-odds bet is not in play on the come-out roll, though the come bet itself is. (The free odds on the don't come, pass and don't pass bets are always in play.)

Double Odds

Some casinos offer double odds as an inducement to the bettor. These work just like the odds bets described above except that even more money can be bet on the free odds wager. In the case of double odds, double the money could be wagered on the bet.

Place Bets

These are bets that a particular point number, the 4, 5, 6, 8, 9 or 10, whichever is bet on, will be rolled before a 7 is thrown. The player can make as many place bets as he wants.

Place bets of 4 or 10 are paid at 9 to 5, on 5 or 9 are paid at 7 to 5 and 6 or 8 are paid at 6 to 5. These bets are not in play on the come-out roll.

Big 6 and Big 8

These are bets that the 6 (Big 6) or 8 (Big 8) are rolled before the 7. Winning bets are paid off at even money.

Field Bet

This is a one roll bet that the next roll of the dice will be a number listed in the field box - a 2, 3, 4, 9, 10, 11 or 12. Rolls of 2 and 12 pay double, all others in the box pay even money. Rolls of 5, 6, 7 and 8 are losers. This bet can be made anytime. (In some casino, the 2 or 12 may pay triple.)

Any 7

A bet that the following roll will be a 7. Pays the winner 4 to 1.

Any Craps

A bet that the following roll will be a 2, 3 or 12. Pays 7 to 1.

2 or 12

Can bet either or both. A bet that the next roll will be a 2 (or 12). Pays 30 to 1.

3 or 11

A bet that the 3 or the 11, whichever is chosen, will come up next. Pays 15 to 1.

Horn Bet

A four-way bet that the next roll will be a 2, 3, 11 or 12. Pays off 15 to 1 on the 3 or 11 and 30 to 1 on the 2 or 12. The other three losing chips are deducted from payoff.

HOUSE EDGE IN CRAPS CHART

Bet		Payoff	House Edge
Pass or Come		1 to 1	1.41%
Don't Pass, Don't Come		1 to 1	1.40%
Free Odds Bets*	***		0.00%
Single Odds**	***		0.8%
Double Odds**	***		0.6%
Place 4 or 10		9 to 5	6.67%
Place 5 or 9		7 to 5	4.00%
Place 6 or 8		7 to 6	1.52%
Field		2 to 1 on 12	
		1 to 1 other #s	5.56%
Field		3 to 1 on 12	
		1 to 1 other #s	2.78%
Any Craps		7 to 1	11.11%
Any 7		4 to 1	16.67%
2 or 12		30 for 1	16.67%
'		30 to 1	13.89%
3 or 11		15 for 1	16.67%
'		15 to 1	11.11%
Hardways 4 or 10		8 for 1	11.11%
6 or 8		10 for 1	9.09%

*The free odds bet by itself
**The free odds bet combined with pass, don't pass,
  come and don't come wagers
***The payoffs on the free odds portion of the bets vary.
See discussion under free odds for their listing.

Hardways

Whenever the numbers 4, 6, 8 and 10 are rolled as doubles, the roll is said to be thrown hardways.

Betting hardways is a wager that the doubled number chosen comes up before a 7 is thrown, or before the number is thrown easy (not as a double).

Bets on hardways 6 or 8 pay 9 to 1, and on hardways 4 or 10, pay 7 to 1.

Right and Wrong Betting

Betting with the dice, pass line and come betting, is called **right betting,** while betting against the dice, making don't pass and don't come bets, is called **wrong betting**.

Betting right or wrong are equally valid methods of winning, with equivalent odds, and the choosing of either way, or alternating between the two, is merely a matter of personal style.

WINNING STRATEGY

There are many bets available to the craps player, but to get the best chances of beating the casino, you must make only the bets which give the casino the least possible edge.

You can see from the chart that bets vary in house edge from the combined pass line: double odds wager where the house has but a 0.6% edge to the horn bet where the house edge can be as high as 16.67%!

To win at craps, make only pass and come bets backed up by free-odds wagers or don't pass and don't come bets, and back these wagers up with free-odds bets.

These bets reduce the house edge to the absolute minimum, a mere 0.8% in a single odds game or 0.6%

in a double odds game if this strategy is followed.

The house edge on the rest of the bets are too large to be incorporated into a winning strategy, and bettors making these bets will soon find themselves drained of their bankroll. These exotic bets seem like a lot of fun, but you'll probably have a lot more fun winning, so stay away.

By concentrating our bets this way, we're making only the best bets available at craps, and in fact, will place the majority of our bets on wagers the casino has absolutely no edge on whatsoever!

This is the best way to give yourself every chance of beating the casino when the dice are hot and you've got bets riding on winners.

Try to keep two or three points going at one time by making pass and come bets if you're a right bettor, or don't pass and don't come bets if you're a wrong bettor and back all these bets with the full free odds available.

Money management is very important in craps, for money can be won or lost rapidly. However, try to catch that one good hot streak, and if you do, make sure you walk away a winner.

GLOSSARY

Any Craps - A bet that the following roll will be a 2, 3 or 12.

Any Seven - A bet that the following roll will be a 7.

Back Line - Refers to the don't pass area.

Bar the 12 - A term found in the don't pass and don't come areas which makes the roll of a 12 (in some casinos the 2) a standoff.

Big 6 & Big 8 - A bet that the 6, or the 8, whichever is bet on, will be thrown before a 7 is rolled.

Boxman - Casino executive who supervises the craps table from a seat between the two standing dealers.

Buy Bets - A player option to buy a point number and get paid at the correct odds. However, a 5% commission must be paid to buy the number.

Call Bet - A verbal bet that a wager is working. Disallowed in many casinos by the indication "No Call Bets" on the layout.

Center Bets - see **Proposition Bets**.

Come Bet - A bet that the dice will win, or pass. Works just like a pass bet except that it can only be made after a point is established.

Come-Out Roll - The roll made before any point has been established.

Coming Out - A term to designate that a new come-out roll is about to happen.

Correct Odds - The mathematical likelihood that a bet will be a winner, expressed in odds.

Crap Out - The roll of a 2, 3 or 12 on a come-out roll, an automatic loser for pass line bettors.

Craps - Term used to denote a 2, 3 or 12. Also the name of the game.

Craps-Eleven - A one roll bet combining the Any Craps and 11.

Dealer - The casino employee who works directly with the player and who handles all monetary transactions and bets.

Don't Come Bet - A bet made against the dice. The bet works just like the don't pass except that it can only be made after a point is established.

Don't Pass - A bet made on the come-out roll only, that the dice will lose.

Double Odds Bet - A free-odds bet that allows the player to bet double his line wager as a right bettor, and double the line payoff as a wrong bettor.

Easy, Easy Way - The throw of a 4, 6, 8 or 10 other than as a pair, such as 1-5, *6 the easy way*.

Even-Money - The payoff of one dollar for every dollar bet.

Field Bet - A one-roll bet that the next roll will be a number in the field box - 2, 3, 4, 9, 10, 11 or 12.

Free-Odds Bets - A bet made in conjunction with the line, come and don't come bets, that is made after the establishment of a point. The house has no advantage on these wagers.

Front Line - Refers to the pass line.

Hardway Bet - A sequence bet that the hardway number, the 4, 6, 8 or 10 will come up in doubles before it comes up easy, or before a 7 is thrown.

Hardway - The throw of a 4, 6, 8 or 10 as a pair, such as 3-3; *6 the hardway*.

Hop Bet - A bet that the next roll will be a specific combination. Usually not found on the layout.

Horn Bet - A one roll bet that the next throw will be a 2, 3, 11 or 12.

Inside Numbers - The place numbers 5, 6, 8, 9.

Lay Bet - A wager made by wrong bettors that a 7 will show before the point number is thrown.

Line Bet - Refers to a pass or don't pass bet.

Marker Buck - Round disk used to mark either the point or to indicate that no point is yet established. Also called **Puck**, or **Marker Puck**.

Odds Bet - See **Free-Odds Bet**.

Off - A designation that a bet is not working on a particular roll.

On - A designation that a bet is working on a particular roll.

One Roll Bet - A bet whose outcome is determined on the very next throw of the dice.

Outside Numbers - The numbers 4, 5, 9 and 10.

Pass, Pass Line - A bet made on the come-out roll only, that the dice will pass, or win.

Payoff, House Payoff - The amount of money the casino pays the player on a winning bet.

Place Bet - A wager that a particular number, the 4, 5, 6, 8, 9 or 10, will be rolled before a 7.

Point, Point Number - The throw of a 4, 5, 6, 8, 9 or 10 on the come-out roll becomes the point.

Proposition or Center Bets - The bets located in the center of the layout.

Right Bettors - Players betting that the dice will pass. Pass and come bettors.

Sequence Bet- A bet whose outcome may take a succession of rolls to be determined.

Seven-Out - The roll of a 7 after a point has been established, a loser for pass line bettors.

Shoot - A progression of rolls ending on either an immediate decision on the come-out roll, or the sevening-out after a point had been established.

Shooter - The player throwing the dice.

Single Odds - A free-odds bet that allows the player to bet equal to his line wager as a right bettor, and equal the payoff as a wrong bettor.

Stickman - Casino employee who controls the dice with a hooked stick, calls the game and controls the proposition bet area.

Toke or Tip - A gratuity given or bet for the dealer.

Unit - Bet size used as a standard of measurement.

Working - Designation that a bet is on or in play.

Wrong Bettors - Players betting that the dice won't pass. Don't pass and don't come bettors.

Yo-Leven - Slang term for the roll of an 11.

WINNING SLOTS

The allure of slot machine play has hooked millions of players looking to reap the rewards of a big jackpot!

The Machines

There are basically two types of slot machines. The first type, the **Straight Slots**, pays winning combinations according to the schedule listed on the machine itself. These payoffs never vary.

The second type of machines are called **Progressive Slots.** These too have a standard set of payoffs listed on the machine itself, but in addition, and what makes for exciting play, is the big jackpot which progressively gets larger as every coin is played This jackpot total is posted above the machine and can accumulate to enormous sums of money!

The Basics

Slots are easy to play. Machines generally take anywhere from 1 to 5 coins, and all one needs to do is insert the coins into the machine, pull the handle and see what Lady Luck brings.

There are many types of slot machine configurations but all work according to the same principles -

put the money in the slots and pull!

For example, some machines will pay just the middle horizontal line, while others, may pay on any winning combination not only left to right, but diagonally as well. Other combinations exist as well.

Often, the number of lines the machine will pay on depends on the amount of coins deposited. One coin only may pay the middle line, a second coin will pay the top line as well, a third coin - the bottom line, a fourth - the diagonal and a fifth - the other diagonal.

More winning rows does not necessarily equate to better odds of winning. The odds are built into the machine and no amount of lines played will change them. The most important factor is how loose or tight the machines are set by the casino - that is what determines the odds facing a slots player.

Your best method is simply to play the machine most suited to your personal style.

SLOTS STRATEGY

The most important concept in slots is to locate the machines with the loosest setting, or with progressive machines, to play only the machines with the highest progressive setting.

Some casinos advertise slots with returns as high as 97% to the player, others, even as high as 99%! Obviously, the player stands a much better chance of winning at these places than others where a standard return of only 84% might be the norm. On some machines, players may not even get an 84% return.

In general, the poorer paying machines will be located in areas where the casino or slots proprietor hopes to grab a few of the bettor's coins as he passes through an area or waits on a line.

Airport terminals, restaurant and show lines, bathrooms and the like tend to have smaller returns.

On the other hand, casinos that specialize in slots and serious slots areas within a casino will have better payoffs. These casinos view slots as an important income, and in order to keep regular slots customers, these bettors must hear those jackpot bells ringing - after all, winning is contagious!

Some machines are set to pay better than others, and these slots will be mixed in with poorer paying ones, so its always a good idea to look for the hot machine. Better yet, ask the change girls. They spend all day near the slots and know which machines tend to return the most money.

When you hit a good jackpot, make sure you set your stop-loss limit. This guarantees that you walk away a winner!

Jackpot!

WINNING KENO

The chance to win $50,000 from a tiny $1.00 bet, and the ease of playing from anywhere in the casino, makes keno a popular gambling game wherever available.

The Keno Ticket

There are 80 numbered squares on a keno ticket which correspond exactly to the 80 numbered balls in the keno cage. A player may choose anywhere from one number to fifteen numbers to play, and does so by marking an "x" on the keno ticket for each number or numbers he or she so chooses.

The Basics

Twenty balls are drawn each game, and appear as lighted numbers on the keno screens. If enough numbers have been correctly picked or **caught**, you have a winner, and the chart will show the payoff. The more numbers that come up, the greater the winnings.

Winnings are determined by consulting the payoff chart each casino provides.

Bets are usually made in .70 or $1.00 multiples, though other bets may apply, and a player may play as many tickets as he or she desires.

Marking the Ticket

The amount being wagered on a game should be placed in the box marked *Mark Price Here* in the upper right hand corner of the ticket.

Leave out dollar or cents signs though. $1 would be indicated by simply placing 1- and 70 cents by .70. Of course, any amount up to the house limit can be wagered.

Underneath this box is a column of white space. The number of spots selected for the game is put here. If six spots were selected on the ticket, mark the number 6, if fifteen numbers, mark 15.

This type of ticket, which is the most common one bet, is called a **straight ticket.**

5 Spot Straight Ticket

33

Split Tickets

A player may also play as many combinations as he chooses. **Split tickets** allow a player to bet two or more combinations in one game. This is done by marking two sets (or more) of from 1-15 numbers on a ticket and separating them by either a line, or by circling the separate groups. Numbers may not be duplicated between the two sets.

On split tickets in which several games are being played in one, the keno ticket should be marked as follows. In addition to the x's indicating the numbers, and the lines or circles showing the groups, the ticket should clearly indicate the number of games being played.

Split Ticket

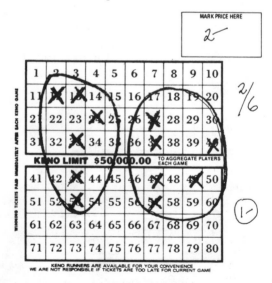

34

For example, a split ticket playing two groups of six spots each would be marked 2/6 in the column of white space. The 2 shows that two combinations are being played, and the 6 shows that six numbers are being chosen per game.

If $1 is being bet per combination, we would put a 1- and circle it underneath the slashed numbers to show this, and of course, in the *Mark Price Here* box, we would enter 2, to show $2 is being bet - $1 on each combination.

Combination Tickets

Combination tickets allow the player to combine groups of numbers in all sorts of ways and the player would bet one unit for each combination possible.

For example, the player can indicate groups of two, three and four numbers on a ticket. Using all possible combinations, he can play the game as a 2-spot, 3-spot, 4-spot, 5-spot (2 + 3), 6-spot (2-spot + 4 spot), 7-spot (3-spot + 4 spot) and 9-spot (2-spot, 3-spot and 4-spot) for a total of a seven unit bet.

The groups chosen on combination tickets should all be clearly marked in the white space on the right of the keno ticket. In the above example of a combination ticket, we would mark 1/2, 1/3, 1/4, 1/5, 1/6, 1/7 and 1/9, showing that one combination is being played on each of these groupings.

If $1 was bet per grouping, we would circle 1- underneath, just like on the way ticket. Seven combinations by $1 per group, and we have a total bet of $7. This gets marked as 7- in the *Mark Price Here* area.

Way Tickets

Way tickets combine at least three groups of equal

numbers which can be combined in several ways as straight ticket combinations. For example, three groups of five can be circled giving the player in actuality three groups of ten-spots. This ticket would be bet as three games.

In this example, the ticket would have 3/10 marked on the side to show that three groups of 10 are being played.

King Tickets

Finally, there is the **king ticket** in which one number is circled by itself, called the **king**, and used in combination with other circled groups on the ticket.

For example, along with the "king," a player circles a group of two numbers and three numbers. The game can now be played as a 3-spot (king + 2-spot), 4-spot (king + 3-spot), 5-spot (2-spot + 3-spot) and a 6-spot (king + 2-spot + 3-spot) for a total of 4 ways. If each game cost $1, than this ticket would cost $4 to play.

King tickets are marked similarly to the way and split tickets, showing the combinations played, the amount bet per grouping and the total bet.

Winning Strategy

Keno is a game that should not be played seriously for the odds are prohibitively against the player. The house edge is typically well over 20% and higher - daunting odds if one wants to win in the long run.

One thing to look out for is that some casinos offer better payoffs on the big win than others, so a little shopping might get you closer to a bigger payoff.

For example, some casinos will pay $40,000 if you catch all the numbers while another may pay just $25,000. Why not play for the $40,000?

Keno is a great game to test out your lucky numbers. Picking birth dates, anniversaries, license plate numbers and the like offer a big pool of possibilities to see which ones will really pay off.

Do you play the same numbers and combinations every game or switch around when one set fails? And what if the original set then wins, or if you didn't switch and the numbers you would have played won? Oh, the heartaches!

If you know your lucky numbers, you may just give them a whirl and see if you can't walk away with a $50,000 bonanza!

GLOSSARY

Caller - Casino employee who calls each number as it's drawn

Catch - To match one or more numbers on ticket with those drawn. *To catch three numbers.*

Combination Ticket - A ticket combining groups of numbers to form two or more winning possibilities.

Draw - The random drawing of 20 numbers in a game.

Duplicate Ticket - The ticket marked in India ink by the keno writer reflecting the numbers bet and returned to the player.

Keno Balls - The 80 numbered balls, 1-80, of which 20 are randomly drawn in a keno game.

Keno Board - The lit board which indicates the 20 numbers drawn in a game.

Keno Lounge - The area set aside for keno in a casino.

Keno Runners - The casino employees who roam the casino area outside the keno lounge and take bets on keno games.

Keno Writer - The employee who processes keno bets and issues duplicates.

King - Also **king number**. The roaming number on a king ticket which is combined other groups or kings to make combinations in a game.

King Ticket - A combination type ticket using the king number.

Original Ticket - The original ticket filled out by the player and held by the casino. Also **inside ticket**.

Multi-Game Ticket - A ticket recorded once and played unchanged for one or more games.

Punch-Outs - Also **draw ticket**. Special ticket with holes punched-out reflecting the 20 drawn numbers in a game.

Rate Card - The booklet issued by a casino showing the bets and their payoffs

Special Tickets - Tickets with different prices and payoffs from those in the rate card.

Split Ticket - A combination-type ticket with two or more groups of numbers.

Spots - The marked numbers on a ticket.

Straight Ticket - A ticket where 1-15 spots are selected without combinations. Also basic ticket.

Way Ticket - A combination-type ticket with at least three different groups of equal numbers.

Writer - See **Keno Writer**.

WINNING POKER

Poker is one of the greatest games ever invented. No other game involves the ingenious combination of skill, luck and psychology in such a fascinating blend.

The Basics

Poker is played with a standard 52 card deck and can support anywhere from two to usually a maximum of about eight or nine players. Cards are valued in descending order, with the ace being the most powerful, then the king, the queen, the jack, the 10 and so on down to the lowly deuce.

The four suits - spades, diamonds, hearts, clubs - have no intrinsic value in the determination of winning hands, and, as we shall see, it is not the value of individual cards but the combination of cards together which determine winning and losing hands.

Poker Variations

While there are hundreds of variations of this great game, the most popular styles played are seven card high stud, high-low stud, lowball: draw poker and seven card stud, hold'em, jacks or better and anything opens.

Though poker is usually played as high poker, there are also low poker and wild card poker variations.

RANKS OF POKER HANDS

First let's go over the ranks of the hands in ascending order, from the lowest ranking to the highest.

We'll employ the following commonly used symbols: ace = A, king = K, queen = Q, Jack = J, and all others by their numerical symbol, such as 9 = nine, and 8 = eight, and so on.

RANKS OF POKER HANDS

High Card - When no other cards are matched, the high card in the hand, determines the strength.

One Pair - Two cards of equal value are called a pair, such as 7-7 or K-K.

Two Pair - Two sets of paired cards, such as 3-3 and 10-10.

Three of a Kind - Three cards of equal value, such as 9-9-9.

Straight - Five cards in numerical sequence, such as 3-4-5-6-7 or 10-J-Q-K-A. The ace can be counted as the highest card or the lowest card in a straight, however, it may not be a middle card. (Q-K-A-2-3 is not a straight.)

Flush - Any five cards of the same suit, such as five hearts.

Full House - Three of a kind and a pair together, such as 2-2-2-J-J.

Four of a kind - Four cards of equal value, such as K-K-K-K.

Straight Flush - A straight all in the same suit, such as 7-8-9-10-J, all in spades.

Royal Flush - 10-J-Q-K-A, all in the same suit.

Wild Card Poker

In some games players will designate a card or cards as *wild*. **Wild cards** can take on any value or suit at the holder's discretion - even as a duplicate of a card already held. The only difference in wild card rankings in wild poker from the standard game is that the highest hand is five of a kind. All other ranking are the same.

Low Poker Rankings

In low poker, the ranking of hands are the opposite to that of high poker, with the lowest hand being the most powerful. The ace is considered the lowest and therefore the most powerful card, with the hand 5 4 3 2 A being the best low total possible.

Play of the Game

Most private and virtually all casino games require an **ante,** a uniform bet placed by all players into the pot before the cards are dealt. The size of the ante is prearranged by the players, or in a casino is set by the house.

The cards are dealt clockwise, left to right, and likewise play proceeds in this fashion, beginning in the first round with either the player sitting to the im- mediately left of the dealer, or in some stud games, with either the high or low card showing, as the case may be, opening play.

In later rounds though, the first player to act will vary depending upon the variation played. We'll look at each game in turn.

Except for the times when a bet is mandatory, as is usually the case in the initial round of play, the first player to act in a betting round has three options: He can **bet** and does so by placing money in the pot, he can **check** or **pass**, make no bet at all and pass play on to the next player; or he can **fold** or **go out**, throw away his cards and forfeit play in the hand.

However, once a bet is placed, a player no longer has the option of checking his turn. To remain an active player, he must either **call the bet**, place an amount of money into the pot equal to the bet; or he can **raise** (**call and raise**), call the bet and make an additional bet.

If a player doesn't want to call the bets and raises that have preceded him, then he must fold and go out of play. Each succeeding player, clockwise and in turn, is faced with the same options: calling, folding or raising.

When play swings around to the original bettor, he or she must call any previous raises to continue as an active player as must any subsequent players who have raises due, or he must fold. A player may raise again if the raise limit has not been reached.

The number of raises permitted vary with the game, but generally, casino games limit the raises to three or five total in any one round, except when only two players are left, when unlimited raising is allowed. Most private games allow unlimited raising.

A player may only raise another player's bet or raise, not his own bet.

Play continues until the last bet or raise is called by all active players, and no more bets or raises are due any player. The betting round is now completed and over.

Some games use a **blind**, a mandatory bet that must be made by the first player to act in the opening round of play, regardless of cards.

Check and raise, a player's raising of a bet after already checking in a round, is usually not allowed in private games, though many casino games permit it.

Betting Limits (Limit Poker)

Betting in poker is often structured in a two-tiered level, such as $1-$2, $1-$3, $5-$10, $10-$20 and $30-$60. When the lower limit of betting is in effect, for example in a $5-$10 game, all bets and raises must be in $5 increments, and when the upper range is in effect, all bets and raises must be in $10 increments.

We'll show when these are in effect for the individual games.

Table stakes is the rule in casino and almost all private poker games, and states that a player's bet or call of a bet may not exceed the amount of money he has in front of him.

A tapped-out player can still receive cards until the showdown and play for the original pot, but can no longer take part in the betting, and has no part in the **side pot** in which all future monies in this hand are placed by the active remaining players.

Pot limit and **no limit** are betting structures used in high stakes poker. **Pot limit** games allow the player to bet any amount up to the current size of the pot while the maximum bet in **no limit** is limited only by the table stakes rule.

Most poker games played are limit poker.

The **showdown** is the final act in a poker game, after all betting rounds are concluded, where remaining players reveal their hands to determine the winner. The player with the best hand at the showdown wins all the money in the pot. In the unlikely event of a tie, then the pot is split evenly among the winners.

If only one player remains in the game at any time, there is no showdown and the remaining player automatically collects the pot.

The biggest difference between casino poker and private poker games is that the dealer in a casino game is not a player as he would be in a private game, and that the casino dealer receives a **rake**, a small cut of the action for his services.

Understanding the Rules of the Game

Though poker is basically the same game played anywhere, rules vary from game to game. Before playing, know the answers to the following questions:
1. What are the betting limits?
2. Is "check and raise" allowed?
3. Are antes and blinds used, and if so, how much?
4. What are the maximum number of raises allowed?
5. When playing a casino game, the additional question, "How much is the rake? should be asked.

DRAW POKER VARIATIONS

All bets before the draw in draw poker games, high or low, are in the lower tier of the betting limits when a two-tiered structure such as $1-$2 or $5-$10 are being used, and in the upper limit after the draw is completed.

Draw Poker: Jacks or Better

Each player is dealt five cards face down, and their identity is known only to him. There are two betting rounds. The first occurs before the **draw**, when players have an opportunity to exchange up to three unwanted cards for new ones, or up to four cards, if the remaining card is an ace. (Casinos allow players to exchange all five cards if desired.)

The second round of betting occurs after the draw.

Before the draw, the player immediately to the dealer's left opens the play. To open betting in jacks or better, a player must have a hand with a minimum ranking of a pair of jacks, though if a player has that hand, he does not have to open.

The first player to act must check if he cannot open betting as must all subsequent players in turn. Once an opening bet is made, any player regardless of his hand's value, can call or raise.

If all players check on the opening round, the cards are collected and reshuffled by the next player in turn.

The draw occurs after the first betting round is completed with each remaining player, proceeding clockwise, drawing in turn. The second round of betting follows the draw, and once completed, the showdown occurs.

Draw Poker: Anything Opens

This variation is played exactly the same as in jacks or better except that any hand, regardless of the strength, may open the betting.

Lowball: Draw Poker

In this game, sometimes spelled loball, the lowest hand wins. The ace being the lowest value is the best card, and the hand 5 4 3 2 A, called a **wheel** or **bicycle**, is the best hand.

In lowball, the high card counts in determining the value of a hand: the lower the high card, the better the hand. When the high cards of competing hands are equivalent, the next highest cards are matched up, and the lowest value of these matched cards determines the winner. Thus, the hand 8 6 4 3 2 is a stronger total than 8 7 3 2 A.

When competing hands are the same, the hand is a tie and the pot is split.

Straights and flushes are not relevant in lowball and do not count.

Players may draw as many cards as they want at the draw, exchanging all five cards if so desired.

There are two betting rounds, one before the draw and one after, and then there is the showdown, where the lowest hand collects the plot.

SEVEN CARD STUD POKER VARIATIONS

In each variation, players form their best five card combination out of the seven dealt to produce their best hand.

In seven card high stud, the highest ranking hand remaining wins the pot. In seven card low, the lowest hand wins.

And in high-low stud, players vie for either the highest ranking or lowest ranking hands, with the best of each claiming half the pot; or players can go for the high-low pot and risk all to win all.

In each variation, players receive three initial cards, two face down and one face up. This marks the beginning of the first betting round. The following three cards are dealt face up, one at a time, with a betting round accompanying each card.

The last card, the seventh, comes *down and dirty*, and is the third and last closed card received by the players.

All remaining players now hold three **hole cards** (hidden from the other players view) and four open cards. These are their final cards. One more round of betting ensues and then the showdown occurs.

In high and high low stud, the highest ranking open hand opens betting each round (except in casino play where the lowest ranking card opens play on the first round only).

In seven card low private games, the lowest open card opens and must make a mandatory bet while in the casino game the highest open card makes the required wager. Thereafter, in both games, the lowest ranking hand opens play.

The showdown in seven card high-low stud can be played either as **cards speak**, where players simply reveal their cards at the showdown with the best low and the best high splitting the pot, the game played in the Nevada casinos, or it can be played as declaration, which is predominantly played in private games.

In **declaration**, players simultaneously declare at the showdown whether they're going for the high, the low or the high-low. Usually this is done by hiding colored chips in the hand - white chips being a low declaration, blue chips for high and red chips for high-low.

Of the players who declared "high," the best high hand wins half the pot and for low the best low hand takes the other half. Players that declare high-low must win both, the high and the low, or they forfeit the entire pot.

HOLD 'EM

In this game, best associated with free-wheeling poker, players receive two face down cards and combine these with five face-up community cards pooled in the middle to form their best five card hand.

Altogether, hold 'em has four betting rounds, beginning with the initial deal where all players receive two face down hole cards.

The player to the left of the dealer must make a mandatory opening bet in the opening round. Subsequent players must either call (or raise) to play, or they must fold.

Once the initial betting round is over, it is time for the **flop**. Three cards are turned face up in the center of the table and this is followed by the second round of betting.

The initial opener begins play in this and all subsequent rounds, or if he has dropped out of play, the next active player to his left.

Two more open cards, one at a time, will be dealt face up in the center of the table, with a round of betting following each, and then the showdown where the highest ranking hand wins, or if all opponents have folded, then the last remaining player takes the pot.

GLOSSARY

Ace - The highest ranking card in high poker; in lowball, the lowest and therefore most valuable card.

Action - Betting.

Active Player - Player still in competition for the pot.

Ante - Uniform bet placed into the pot by players before the cards are dealt.

Ante-up - A call for a player or players to put their antes into the pot.

Bet - Money wagered and placed into the pot

Bicycle - In lowball, the A 2 3 4 5 - the best possible hand. Also called a **Wheel**.

Blind - A mandatory bet made on the first round of betting regardless of the cards held. Also, the player making that bet.

Blind Bet - The blind bet itself. Also, a bet placed without looking at one's cards.

Bluff - The act of betting heavily on an inferior hand for the purpose of intimidating opposing players into folding and making the bluffer a winner by default.

Buy-In - The amount of cash a player uses to buy chips for play.

Call - To bet an amount equal to a previous bet on a current round of betting. Also known as **Calling a Bet** or **Seeing a Bet**.

Check - The act of not betting and passing the bet option to the next player while still remaining an active player. Players cannot check when a bet has been made. Also called **Pass**.

Check and Raise - A player's raising of a bet after already checking in that round. Usually not permitted in private games.

Cut - The amount of money taken out of the pot by the house as its fee for running a game. Also called **House Cut**, **Vigorish** and the **Rake**. The cut is also the act of separating the cards into two piles and restacking them in reverse order.

Dealer - The player or casino employee who shuffles the cards and deals them out to the players.

Dealer's Choice - A rule where the current dealer chooses the poker variation to be played.

Deuce - A card term for the two of any suit.

Down - A card dealt with its pips face down so that its value is known only to its holder. Cards dealt face down are called **Downcards**, or **Closed Cards**.

Draw - The exchange of cards allowed after the first round of betting in draw poker variations.

Draw Poker - Form of poker where all cards are

dealt closed - seen only by the holder of those cards.

Face - The side of a card exposing its value.

Face Down - When the side of a card identifying its value faces the table and is therefore hidden from public view. Face down cards are also known as **Downcards** or **Closed Cards**.

Face Up - When the side of a card identifying its value is exposed and can be viewed by all players. Cards dealt face up are also called **Open Cards**.

Flop - In hold 'em, the first three cards simultaneously dealt face up for common use.

Flush - A hand containing five cards of the same suit.

Fold - The withdrawal of further play in a hand. Also referred to as **Going Out**.

Four-of-a-Kind - A hand containing four cards of identical value, such as K K K K, four Kings.

Full House - A hand consisting of three-of-a-kind and a pair, such as 7 7 7 K K.

Hand - The cards a player holds; the best five cards a player can present.

High Poker - Poker variations where high hand wins.

Hole Card - Card held by a player whose value is hidden from other players.

Joker - The "53rd" card in a deck bearing the image of a joker or clown. Sometimes used as a wild card.

Limit Poker - Poker in which the maximum bet size is set at fixed amounts.

Low Poker - Poker form where lowest hand wins.

Misdeal - A deal deemed illegal and invalid.

No Limit - Poker in which the maximum bet allowed is limited only by the amount of money the bettor has on the table.

Opener - The player making the first bet in a betting round. The bet itself.

Pass - see **Check**.

Pat Hand - In draw poker, a hand to which no cards are drawn; also infers an excellent hand.

Picture Card - The jack, queen or king.

Pot - The sum total of all antes and bets placed in the center of the table by players during a poker hand and collected by the winner or winners.

Pot Limit - A rule that the amount of the largest bet can be no more than the current size of the pot.

Raise - A bet which equals a bet made previously in the round, plus an additional bet.

Re-raise - A bet equalling a previous bet and raise, plus an additional bet.

Rake - see **Cut**.

Royal Flush - An A K Q J 10 of the same suit. The highest ranking hand in poker.

Showdown - The final act of a poker game, where remaining players reveal their hands to determine the winner of the pot.

Stand Pat - In draw poker, to draw no cards.

Straight - A sequence of five consecutive cards of mixed suits, such as 4 5 6 7 8

Straight Flush - A sequence of five consecutive cards in the same suit, such as 5 6 7 8 9 of spades.

Stud Poker - Variation of poker where one or more cards are visible to the other players.

Table Stakes - A rule that a player's bet or call of a bet is limited to the amount of money he or she has on the table in front of him.

Trips - Three-of-a-kind.

Up - A card dealt with its pips face up so that its value can be viewed by all players. Cards dealt face up are called **Upcards**.

Wild Card - Cards that can be given any value, even as a duplicate of a card already held.

WINNING BACCARAT

Baccarat is a game that combines the allure and glamour of European tradition with relatively low house odds for the average player, 1.17% in the Banker's position and 1.36% in the Player's spot.

Introduction

Despite the rich tradition and the glamour attached to the game, baccarat can be played by anyone. There's no need to bet mini-fortunes or even to play at high stakes. It is a leisurely game, and in the versions played in the Nevada and American casinos, an easy one as well. There are no decisions to make save for how much you want to bet and which position, Player or Banker, you decide to back.

If you're intimidated by the big tables with the tuxedoed dealers and the aura of big money, the mini-baccarat tables which are tucked in among the blackjack tables can be a good place to begin play and become accustomed to the game.

The low casino edge makes baccarat a perfect place to luxuriate in style, playing this centuries-old game in the grand tradition!

The Baccarat Layout

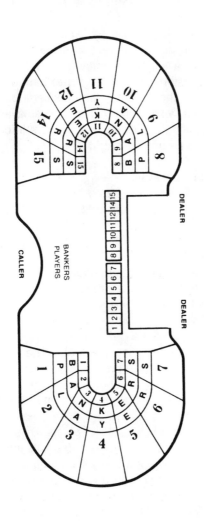

Baccarat Around the World

Baccarat in its different varieties can be found in casinos around the world.

The version played in Nevada casinos is called **baccarat/chemin de fer** or **Nevada style** baccarat while Atlantic City calls it simply **baccarat.** Elsewhere in the world this version is known as **punto banco.**

In Europe, chemin de fer and baccarat banque are quite popular, while mini-baccarat, a smaller version of punto banco is found more and more in casinos in the U.S. and around the world.

The Basics of Play

Baccarat is a simple game to play even for beginners, for the **dealer** or **croupier**, directs all the action according to fixed rules.

Baccarat is played with from six to eight decks of cards dealt out of a shoe. Bets must be placed before the cards are dealt and are made by placing the chips in the appropriate box, **Banker** or **Player**, located in front of the bettor on the layout.

No matter how many players are betting in a game, only two hands will be dealt; one for the Banker position and one for the Player position. The exception is the baccarat banque version, where there are two Player positions instead of one.

Cards numbered 2 to 9 are counted according to their face value, a 2 equals 2 points, an Ace equals one point and a 7 equals 7 points. The 10, Jack, Queen and King have a value of 0 points and have no effect when adding up the points in a hand.

Points are counted by adding up the value of the cards. However, hands totaling 10 or more points, have the first digit dropped so that no hand contains a total of greater than 9 points.

For example, two nines (18) is a hand of 8 points and a 7 5 (12) is a hand of 2 points.

The hand with the closest total to 9 is the winner, while the worst score is zero, called **baccarat**. A tie is a standoff or push, neither hand wins.

There are two opposing sides, the **Player** and the **Banker**, and initially, after the betting is done, each side will receive two cards. Bettors may generally wager on either hand.

A dealt total of 8 or 9 points is called a **natural**, and no additional cards will be drawn. It is an automatic win unless the opposing hand has a higher natural (a 9 vs. an 8), or the hand is a tie. A total of 8 points is called *le petit*; a total of nine, *le grande*.

On all other totals, the drawing of an additional card depends strictly on established rules of play and will be handled by the croupier. There is never more than one card drawn to a hand in any case.

The Player's hand will be acted upon first, and then the Banker's.

Let's sum up the rules for drawing a third card or not in baccarat and than we'll show the rules in chart form for both the Banker and Player positions.

Situation 1 - Either the Player or the Banker position has a natural 8 or 9. It is an automatic win for the hand with the natural. If both hands are naturals, the higher natural wins. (A natural 9 beats a natural 8.) If the naturals are equal, the hand is a tie.

Situation 2 - If the Player position has a 0-5, Player must draw another card; if a 6-7, the Player must stand.

Situation 3 - If Player stands, than the Banker hand follows the same rules as the Player position - it must draw on totals of 0-5 and stand on 6-7.

Situation 4 - If Player draws, Banker must draw or stand according to the value of the third card dealt as show below in the Banker Rules chart.

BANKER RULES

Banker Two Card Total	Banker Draws When Giving Player This Card	Banker Stands When Giving Player This Card
0 - 2	0-9	
3	0-7, (9*)	8
4	2-7	0-1, 8-9
5	5-7, (4*)	0-3, 8-9
6	6-7	0-5, 8-9
7	Banker Always Stands	
8-9	A Natural - Player Can't Draw	

*In punto banco and mini-baccarat, the drawing of a third card is mandatory, while in chemin de fer, it is an optional draw or stand.

Note that unless the Player has a Natural, the Banker always draws with a total of 0-2.

PLAYER RULES

Two Card Total	Player's Action
0-5*	Draw a Card
6 or 7	Stand
8 or 9	Natural. Banker cannot draw.

*In chemin de fer and baccarat banque, the player has the option to stand or draw on a point total of 5 points only.

The winning hand in baccarat is paid at 1 to 1, **even money**, except in the case of the Banker's position where a 5% commission is charged on a winning hand. Commission is charged because of the inherent edge the Banker position has over the Player position.

With the commission, the Banker edge over the bettor is only 1.17%, quite low by casino standards. The house edge over the Player position is only slightly more, 1.36%.

During actual play, this commission is kept track of on the side by use of chips, and won bets at the Banker position are paid off at even money. This avoids the cumbersome 5% change-giving on every hand. The commission will be collected later; at the end of every shoe, and of course, before the player parts from the game.

Let's now look at the differences in the main versions of baccarat as played in casinos around the world.

Baccarat/Chemin de Fer
(American Style Baccarat - Punto Banco)

The bettor has a choice of betting the Player or **Punto** position, or the Banker or **Banco** position. He or she plays against the house which books all bets and pays winning hands. There are no third card drawing options for either the Banker (Banco) or Player (Punto) position.

The bettor may wager on a **tie bet** - a bad bet that pays off at 9 for 1 (8 to 1) and gives the casino an edge of 14.20%. (This bet is not offered in chemin de fer and baccarat banque.)

In this variation of baccarat, the only decisions a player has to make is whether to bet Banker or Player, and how much he or she wants to bet.

Chemin de Fer

The bettor who plays the Banker position deals the cards and books all bets. The other players oppose the Banker. The Player position has one third card drawing option, and is controlled by the bettor with the highest bet placed. The Banker has two drawing options and plays the hand himself. (See Player and Banker Rules charts.) No tie bet is offered.

The casino acts only in a supervisory capacity and collects its fee as a percentage levy or as an hourly rate charged to the players.

The Banker is decided by either **auction**, where the highest bidder takes the Banker position and puts up his or her bid as the bank, by lot or by acceptance as the bank moves its way around the table.

A bettor may play Banker until he loses a hand or voluntarily gives it up, in which case the next player, clockwise or counterclockwise, according to the house rules, can play Banker, and set his own limit on the bets he will book. A bettor may refuse the bank and pass it on to the next player.

The total amount of money bet against the Banker in a hand is limited by the amount of money in the bank.

Any player who wishes to bet against the entire bank, calls out **"banco,"** and this nullifies the other bets.

Baccarat Banque

The casino deals all cards and books all bets. There are two player (punto) positions on this two-sided layout. These spots are manned by bettors who oppose the banker (banco) position which is always taken by the house. Bettors may wager on either Player position or both.

The Player has one third card drawing option. The Banker has no third card drawing restrictions. (Some casinos apply restrictions on the banker.)

Baccarat a Tout Va
Everything goes baccarat in the two-sided style of Baccarat banque. No maximum limit on bets.

Mini-Baccarat
The same game as Punto Banco except that it's played on a miniature blackjack type table, and that the bettors do not deal the cards.

BACCARAT GAME GUIDE

GAME	PLAYER	BANKER
Punto Banco	Yes	Yes
Mini-Baccarat	Yes	Yes
Chemin De Fer	Yes	Only the bettor play ing the Banker may bet Banker.
Baccarat Banque	Yes*	No

*Can wager on either or both of the player hands.

Yes - Indicates a player may bet the position
No - Indicates a player may not bet the position

GLOSSARY

Baccarat - The gambling card game of French origin. Also, the score of zero.

Baccarat Banque - Variation of chemin de fer.

Banco - The Banker position; In chemin de fer, a bet by a player covering the entire bank.

Banker - One of the two betting positions.

Burned Cards - Cards removed from play without being used.

Chemin De Fer - The European form of Baccarat.

Cover - See **Fade**.

Croupier - Dealer, in French.

Dealer - Person dealing the cards; casino employee running a gambling game; croupier.

Fade - Also **Cover**. Chemin de Fer and Craps term describing the act of betting against the bank.

Natural - A two card count of 8 or 9.

Player - One of the two betting positions. Also called **Punto**. Any bettor wagering in a game.

Punto - The Player position.

Scorecard - See **Tally Sheet**.

Shill - Casino employee hired to sit at game and make game look busy.

Tally Sheet.- Also **scorecard**. Sheet of paper used to record wins, losses and other data from a game.

WINNING ROULETTE

The Basics

The game is enormously popular in Europe where it is favored by royalty and celebrities as well as regular gamblers looking for the thrill of action, and less so in America where the odds of winning are much higher.

Roulette is played with a circular wheel containing 36 numbers from 1 to 36 and a betting layout where players can place their wagers.

The European and American game is pretty much the same besides the use of the French terms in Europe, and of course, the American terms in the United States casinos. However, there are two significant differences.

1. In addition to the 36 numbers on the roulette wheel, the American game has a 0 and 00, while the European game has but one 0.

2. The European game has the en prison and partage rules, options which are greatly beneficial to the player. En prison is not offered in American casinos, though "surrender," partage by a different name, is offered in Atlantic City, and is a beneficial option.

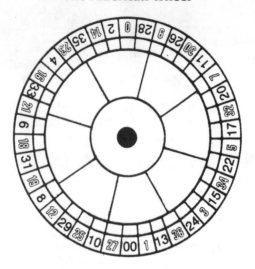

The Play of the Game

Play begins in roulette with the bettors placing their bets on the layout. The wheel will be spun by the dealer or **tourneur** who will also throw the ball in the opposite direction from which the wheel is spinning. When the ball is about to leave the track, the dealer will announce that bets are no longer permitted.

The call of *Faites vos jeux, messieurs* (Make your bets gentlemen) or *Rien ne va plus* (Nothing more goes) are classic in the French speaking casinos.

When the ball has stopped in a slot, the outcome is announced, and the dealer or **croupier**, settles won and lost bets.

Let's now look at the myriad of wagers the roulette player has to choose from.

THE BETS

Roulette offers the player a multitude of possible bets, more than any other casino table game. All in all, there are over 150 possible combinations to bet.

Let's look at those bets now.

Single Number Bet (En Plein)

A single number bet can be made on any number on the layout including the 0 and 00. To do so, place your chip within the lines of the number chosen, being careful not to touch the lines. Otherwise you may have another bet altogether. The winning payoff is 35 to 1.

Split Bet (A Cheval)

Place the chip on the line adjoining two numbers. If either number comes up, the payoff is 17 to 1.

Trio Bet (Transversale)

The chip is placed is placed on the outside vertical line alongside any line of numbers. If any of the three are hit, the payoff is 11 to 1.

4-Number Bet (Carre)

Also called a **square** or **corner** bet. Place the chip on the spot marking the intersection of four numbers. If any of the four come in it is an 8 to 1 payoff.

Quatre Premiere

Only in European roulette. The bet covering the 0, 1, 2 and 3. An 8 to 1 payoff.

5-Number Bet

Only in American roulette. Place the chip at the intersection of the 0, 00 and 2 to cover those numbers plus the 1 and 3. If any of these five come home, the payoff is 6 to 1. In American roulette, it is the only bet not giving the house a 5.26% edge. It's worse - 7.89%!

6-Number Bet (Sixaine)

Also called a **block bet**. Wagers are placed on the outside intersecting line that separates the two sets of three numbers chosen. The payoff is 5 to 1.

Columns Bet (Colonne)

A chip placed at the head of a column, on the far side from the zero or zeros, covers all 12 numbers in the column and has a winning payoff of 2 to 1.

The 0 and 00 are not included in this bet and are losers if they come up.

Dozens Bet (Douzaine)

This is another way to bet 12 numbers, either numbers 1 to 12, 13 to 24 or 25 to 36. On the American layout they're called the **first**, **second** and **third** dozen respectively, and on the French layout, they're known as **P12**, **M12** and **D12**.

The winning payoff as in the column bet is 2 to 1.

EVEN-MONEY BETS

There is one final type of bet, the even money bets: Red-Black (Rouge-Noir), High -Low (Passe-Manque) and Odd-Even (Impair-Pair). Spots for these bets are clearly marked in large, boxes.

Red-Black (Rouge-Noir)

There are 18 black and 18 red numbers. A player may bet either the red or the black and is paid off at 1 to 1 on a winning spin.

The Roulette Layout

1to18 / EVEN / ◇ / ◆ / ODD / 19to36	1st 12	0		00
1to18	1st 12	1	2	3
		4	5	6
EVEN		7	8	9
		10	11	12
◇	2nd 12	13	14	15
		16	17	18
◆		19	20	21
		22	23	24
ODD	3rd 12	25	26	27
		28	29	30
19to36		31	32	33
		34	35	36
		2-1	2-1	2-1

High-Low (Passe-Manque)

Numbers 1-18 may be bet (low) or 19-36 (high). Bets are paid off at 1 to 1.

Odd-Even (Impair-Pair)

There are 18 even numbers and 18 odd numbers. Winning bets are paid at 1 to 1.

ROULETTE PAYOFF CHART
Bets in Roulette

American Name	#	French Name	Payoff
Single Number	1	En Plein	35-1
Split Bet	2	A Cheval	17-1
Trio	3	Transversale	11-1
4-Number (Corner)	4	Carre	8-1
(Not Applicable)	4	Quatre Premiere	8-1
5-Number	5	(Not Applicable)	6-1
6-Number (Block)	6	Sixaine	5-1
Columns Bet	12	Colonne	2-1
Dozens Bet	12	Dozaine	2-1
Red or Black	18	Rouge ou Noir	1-1
High or Low	18	Passe ou Manque	1-1
Odd or Even	18	Impair ou Pair	1-1

column is the amount of numbers covered by the bet.

En Prison, Partage and Surrender

It is on these even number bets (above) where the American and European games really differ. In American roulette, the house automatically wins on these bets when the 0 or 00 is spun. However, in Europe, if the 0 is spun, the en prison rule comes into effect.

The player has two choices now. He or she can either surrender half the bet, called **partage**, or elect to allow the bet to be imprisoned one more spin.

If the spin is won, the bet stays intact and is "released" for the player to do what he or she will. If the spin is lost, so is the bet.

This rule is greatly advantageous to the player, and brings the odds down on these bets to 1.35% in favor of the casino as opposed to the 2.70% on the rest of the bets in the single zero game.

In Atlantic City, the player is offered **surrender** on even money bets only. It works just like partage. If a zero or double zero is spun, the player surrenders half the bet, as opposed to losing all of it as he or she would in Nevada.

The Odds at Roulette

The European game offers the player much better odds than the American game offers its players.

The single zero wheel and en prison rule bring the house edge down to 1.35% on even-money bets and 2.70% on all others in the European game, as opposed to American roulette where the player has to overcome a hefty 5.26% house edge, except in Atlantic City, where bets on even-money wagers only bring the odds down to 2.63%.

The American game also offers the five number bet which is even poorer odds for the player - 7.89%.

CASINO EDGE IN ROULETTE CHART	
American Roulette (Double Zero)	
The 5-Number Bet	7.89%
All Other Bets	5.26%
Atlantic City - Even Money Bets	2.63%
European Roulette (One Zero)	
Even-Money Bets - En Prison Rule	1.35%
All Other Bets	2.70%

GLOSSARY

American Wheel - 0 and 00 Roulette wheel

Ball - Spherical ball spun against wheel's rotation.

Column Bet - A bet on a "column" of 12 numbers.

Combination Bet - Any bet combining two or more individual numbers at once.

Corner Bet - See **Four Number Bet**.

Dozens Bet - A wager on either the first, second or third dozen numbers.

En Prison - A European option on even-money bets, that allows players, when a 0 gets spun, to either give up half their bet or go for another spin and keep the original bet intact .

European Wheel - Roulette wheel using the 0.

Even-Money Bets - The High-Low, Odd-Even and Red-Black bets which pay off at even money.

Five-Number Bet - In American roulette, the bet covering the 1, 2, 3, 0 and 00.

Four-Number Bet - Also **Square** or **Corner Bet**. A bet covering four numbers.

Layout - The betting cloth on which players make their bets.

Odd-Even Bet - An even-money wager on either the odd or the even numbers.

Outside Bet - A wager on either the even-money, dozens or columns bets.

Red-Black Bet - An even-money bet on either the red or black numbers.

Six-Numbers Bet - A bet covering six numbers.

Split Bet - A wager covering two numbers.

Square Bet - See **Four-Number Bet**.

Trio Bet - A bet covering three numbers.

Zero-Double Zero - The numbers on the wheel which account for the casino's edge over the player.

The French Wheel

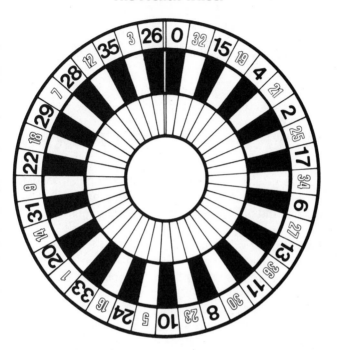

WINNING VIDEO POKER

Video Poker is rapidly becoming the most popular game in the casinos. Decision-making and skill is involved, and proper play can make one a winner!

The Basics of Play

Video poker is basically played as five card draw poker. Five cards will be dealt, and you may exchange as many cards up to that original five as desired. Winnings will be paid according to a pre-set schedule posted on the machine itself.

To play, anywhere from one to five coins are inserted into the machine. Cards will either be dealt automatically, or the player should press the button marked DRAW/DEAL to receive his cards.

Five cards are dealt. The player may keep some or all the cards and does so by pressing the button marked hold underneath the corresponding card he wishes to keep. "HELD" will appear on the screen underneath each card or cards so chosen. If you change your mind, re-press the button, and HELD will disappear, or re-press it again for HELD to reappear.

The DRAW/DEAL button is now pressed and those

cards not chosen to be held will be replaced with new ones. This set of cards is the final hand.

Following are the winning hands in video poker.

WINNING HANDS IN VIDEO POKER

Jacks or Better - Two cards of equal value are called a pair. Jacks or better refers to a pairing of Jacks, Queens, Kings or Aces.

Two Pair - Two sets of paired cards, such as 3-3 and 10-10.

Three of a Kind - Three cards of equal value, such as 9-9-9.

Straight - Five cards in numerical sequence, such as 3-4-5-6-7 or 10-J-Q-K-A. The ace can be counted as the highest card or the lowest card in a straight, however,

Flush - Any five cards of the same suit, such as five hearts.

Full House - Three of a kind and a pair together, such as 2-2-2-J-J.

Four of a kind - Four cards of equal value, such as K-K-K-K.

Straight Flush - A straight all in the same suit, such as 7-8-9-10-J, all in spades.

Royal Flush - 10-J-Q-K-A, all in the same suit.

Keeping or Discarding All Five Cards

A player may keep all five original cards and does so by pushing the hold button under each card and then pressing the DEAL/DRAW button, or he or she may discard all five original cards if desired by pressing the DRAW/DEAL button without having pressed any of the hold buttons.

Winning Hands

If your hand is a winner, the machine will flash "WINNER" at the bottom of the screen and credits will build up in the machine. These credits can either be left in the machine and used for easy play, or they can be retrieved at any time by pressing the CASH OUT button, whereupon the coins will tumble into the well. Winning hands are automatically paid according to the payoffs shown on the machine.

The following chart shows typical payoffs for video poker on a Jacks or Better machine. This machine is known as an **8-5 machine**, so named for the payoffs given on the full house and flush respectively.

PAYOFFS ON JACKS OR BETTER: 8-5 MACHINE					
Coins Played	1	2	3	4	5
Jacks of Better	1	2	3	4	5
Two Pair	2	4	6	8	10
Three of a Kind	3	6	9	12	15
Straight	4	8	12	16	20
Flush	5	10	15	20	25
Full House	8	16	24	32	40
Four of a Kind	25	50	75	100	125
Straight Flush	50	100	150	200	250
Royal Flush	250	500	750	1000	4000

Deuces Wild and Jokers Wild

Besides the Jacks or Better machine discussed above, some video poker machines are played as **deuces wild** or **jokers wild**. Wild cards can be given any value or suit and the machine will interpret wild cards in the most advantageous way for the player.

For example, the hand 2 2 5 6 8 in deuces wild would be a straight, for one 2 can be used as a 7 and the other as either a 9 or 4. The deuces could also be used as eights to give three of a kind, but since the straight is more valuable to the player the machine will see it as a straight.

Wild card machines have different payoff schedules than the jacks or better machines, and these payoffs will start giving credit only on a three of a kind hand or better.

Following is a typical payoff schedule for a deuces wild machine. These payoffs may vary from machine to machine

PAYOFFS ON DEUCES WILD					
Coins Played	1	2	3	4	5
Three of a Kind	1	2	3	4	5
Straight	2	4	6	8	10
Flush	2	4	6	8	10
Full House	3	6	9	12	15
Four of a Kind	4	8	12	16	20
Straight Flush	8	16	24	32	40
Five of a Kind	10	20	30	40	50
Royal Flush (with deuces)	20	40	60	80	100
Four Deuces	200	400	600	800	1000
Royal Flush (no deuces)	250	500	750	1000	4000

Besides the straight machines discussed above, there are progressive machines, as in slots. All payoffs, like the straight machines are fixed except in the case of a royal flush, where this grandaddy pays the accumulated total posted above the machine on the electronic board.

This total slowly, but constantly rises, and on a quarter machine in Las Vegas can rise into the thousands of dollars. When the big money has accumulated, then the game gets more interesting!

WINNING STRATEGY

The big payoff in video poker on the jacks or better machines is for the royal flush - a whopping 4,000 coins are paid for this score when five coins are played.

And on progressive machines, if a full five coins are played, the total could be a great deal higher, possibly as high as $3,000 (12,000 coins) on a quarter machine.

Of course, the royal doesn't come often. With correct strategy, you'll hit one every 30,000+ hands on the average. This doesn't mean, however, that you won't hit one in your very first hour of play!

But meanwhile, you'll be collecting other winners such as straights, full houses and the like, and with proper play, all in all, you can beat the video poker machines.

To collect the full payoff for a royal flush, proper play dictates that you always play the full five coins for each game. Of course, those that want to play less seriously can play any amount of coins from 1 to 5.

The next page shows the correct strategies for the 9-6 Flattops.

(The following strategies are not applicable to the 8-5 Progressives. For full strategy charts on all video poker games including the Progressives, Jokers Wild, Deuces Wild and more, you may want to order the strategy in the back.)

JACKS OR BETTER: 9-6 FLATTOP STRATEGY

1. Whenever you hold <u>four cards to a royal flush</u>, discard the fifth card, even if that card gives you a flush or pair.

2. Keep a <u>jacks or better pair</u> and any higher hand such as a three of a kind or straight over three to the royal. Play the <u>three to a royal</u> over any lesser hand such as a low pair or four flush.

3. With <u>two cards to a royal</u>, keep four straights, four flushes, and high pairs or better instead. Otherwise, go for the royal.

4. Never break up a <u>straight or flush</u>, unless a one card draw gives you a chance for the royal.

5. Keep <u>jacks or better</u> over a four straight or four flush.

6. Never break up a <u>four of a kind</u>, <u>full house</u>, <u>three of a kind</u> and <u>two pair</u> hands. The *rags*, worthless cards for the latter two hands, should be dropped on the draw.

7. The <u>jacks or better pair</u> is always kept, except when you have four cards to the straight or royal flush.

8. Keep <u>low pairs</u> over the four straight, but discard them in favor of the four flushes and three or four to a royal flush.

9. When dealt <u>unmade hands</u>, pre-draw hands with no payable combination of cards, save in order; four to a royal flush and straight flush, three to a royal flush, four flushes, four straights, three to a straight flush, two cards to the royal, two cards jack or higher and one card jack or higher.

10. Lacking any of the above, with no card jack or higher, discard all the cards and draw five fresh ones.

WINNING LOTTO & THE LOTTERY

Lotto and lottery fever has swept the continent, with players from coast to coast looking to cash in on the big jackpot, the dream win that will put them on easy street.

Introduction

While the odds of winning a giant jackpot are overwhelmingly against the player, there are smaller prizes ranging from a few dollars to winnings in the thousands that are within reach, even though overall, the odds of winning are greatly against the players. Still, the main lure of the big jackpot keeps millions playing week after week.

There are three basic types of games; the Instant games, the lotteries, and the lotto games. We'll go over each in turn, and discuss the basic winning strategies involved.

Instant Game

There are a wide variety of instant "scratch-off" games, but all work according to the same principle: the player scratches off the latex covering to reveal possible winners in the form of numbers or pictures. Winners are either paid off on the spot by the vendor, or if the ticket is a big winner, they may be redeemed by the state.

Since players don't choose numbers as they would in the other types of lottery games, there is no real strategy in the instant lotto other than the luck of the draw.

Lottery Games

Lottery games are played as either three-ball or four-ball games, and occur almost nightly in the states offering them. There are separate containers containing 10 balls each, numbered 0-9, and one ball is drawn from each of these chutes. These balls constitute the winning numbers.

In three ball lottery games, players choose three numbers, and in the four ball games, four numbers are chosen. These numbers picked must match the actual balls drawn, *in exact order drawn*, for the tickets to be a winner. For example, if a player chooses 7-0-5, and 7-0-5 is drawn, he's a winner. However, a drawing of 7-5-0 would be a loser on that ticket.

In a three ball game, combinations range form 000-999 with payoffs typically around $500 for the correct numbers drawn, and in a four ball game, from 0000-9999 with payoffs typically around $5,000 for all four numbers hitting.

Lotto Games

Five-ball, Six-ball (Pick Six) and Power Ball games are the most popular lotto games played. Balls are drawn randomly, one at a time, from a bin holding all the balls, until the correct amount of balls have been drawn. This is unlike the lottery, where each ball is drawn from a different container.

In a five ball game, five balls will be drawn. In a six ball game, six balls will be drawn. And in Power Ball, while six balls will be drawn as well, the sixth ball will be taken from a different pool of balls than the first five were drawn. These drawn balls are the ones which determine the winner, and are called the **draw**.

The number of balls in the total pool vary from state to state, with the most common configuration being 6/49 in six ball - six balls drawn out of a pool of 49 balls, numbered 1 through 49.

Games with more numbers in the pool, such as 6/50, are worse for the player for each added ball adds one more chance that a chosen number won't be drawn. Conversely, fewer numbers, such as 6/48, benefit the player, for now each number chosen is more likely to be drawn.

If all numbers a player chooses matches the final draw, then the grand prize is won. However, unlike the lottery, the order of the balls drawn have no relevance on whether the ticket is a winner. If the correct numbers are drawn, regardless of the order, the ticket is a winner. If more than one player chooses the correct numbers, the big win is split among the winners.

There are also other prizes for five, four and even three correct numbers chosen.

The Payoffs

Jackpots reach into the tens of millions of dollars and more with the actual size of the lotto jackpot being determined by the amount of money bet into the total pool by the players participating. The more tickets bought, the higher the jackpot gets until some lucky player or players pick the winning numbers.

If no players have chosen the winning numbers, the jackpot carries over to the next drawing and gets larger and larger as new bets are added to the pool. As jackpots grow, the publicity and resultant betting gets more frenzied, and before you know it, there's a monster jackpot with players from across the country getting in on the action, some to the tune of hundreds or even thousands of bets!

The state keeps a large percentage of the total money bet, usually around 50%, as their profit for running the game with the rest of the money being returned to the winning players.

Winning Strategies

While the Instant Games present no strategic possibilities for players, the three and four ball lotteries, and five and six ball lottos, have players constantly working out the numbers for the best chances of winning.

The basic winning strategies are based on the fact that balls are drawn from the same pool of numbers drawing after drawing, and they look for tendencies or *biases* that can be translated into winnings.

Serious lotto and lottery players keep track of the numbers drawn each time a drawing is held either by hand, or with the assistance of computer programs. They seek to track numbers that either occur often, and in theory, will continue to come up often, or numbers that haven't come up in a while, and are "overdue."

Often, players will come up with many numbers they would like to play, and rather than betting every possibility, which will cost a fortune, they rely on a **wheeling system**, a scientific method of betting a group of numbers in various combinations such that all the desired numbers are bet at a reduced cost while maintaining a high chance of winning should those numbers be drawn.

For example, if a player wants to bet all combinations

of 12 numbers in a six-ball lotto, 924 bets would have to be made to cover all combinations. If each ticket bet costs $1, that's $924 - a lot of wampum for one drawing. However, a good wheeling system can give the player better than an 80% chance of winning by betting just 6 games!

In any case, if you enjoy the lotto and lottery games, keep your bets within reason, for otherwise, the huge house advantage will drain your bankroll fast. But maybe also, you just might hit the big win and we'll see you on the news!

WINNING STRIP POKER

The most exciting card game in the world, strip poker is a way to really liven up an evening. It's a fun game with the allure of many possible outcome!

Introduction

The great thing about strip poker is that unlike the other forms of poker where money is bet and either lost or won, in this game, winning and losing is not measured in material gains and losses, but rather how much enjoyment was had in the play.

If strip poker is played with the right participants, a lot of fun can be had, and everybody comes out a winner. Sounds pretty good? It sure is!

In this section we'll show you the basics of play and the rules, but once that's done, the rest is up to you and the other participants in the game.

Strip Poker Play

Though any form of poker can be used, strip poker is best played as draw poker, using an ante, plus the standard two bets, one before the draw and one after. Other poker forms such as five card stud, or even seven card, have too many betting rounds, and the game will proceed too rapidly.

Strip poker is a game we want to savor!

The game proceeds just as in regular draw poker, with raises and reraises allowed, but with one major difference. The form of currency used is not money or chips, but clothing!

There are important rules in strip poker, just as in any other form of poker, and these must be followed. Only clothing that a person is wearing or has won from previous hands may be bet.

Clothing is defined as shoes, socks, underwear, pants, skirts, shirts, blouses, sweaters, jackets, scarves, ties, belts and the like, but does not include jewelry, contact lenses, glasses and other items of that nature.

Wigs and toupees are subject to debate.

Once an article of clothing has been removed, it may not be put on again. If that article is won back, it may sit in front of the player as his or her winnings, ready to be wagered on another hand, but it goes no further.

Before each deal, every player is required to ante one article of clothing. However, there is a tax that must be paid. Every deal, before the winner collects the pot, one article of clothing will be permanently removed from play and set off to the side.

So slowly, slowly, the game's currency supply will dwindle and the excitement will grow. Poker is a game where mannerisms, called **tells**, can give away an opponent's hand. So make sure your eyes are not just glued to your cards, you'll need to check out the other things going on in the game.

The maximum bet or raise in strip poker is one

piece of clothing and no more than three raises are permitted in any one round.

Finishing the Game

Betting continues in this game guaranteed to improve one's vision (and imagination) until one player has lost all his or her clothing and sits free to the wind, all their clothing having been lost in the fevered play of the game.

At this point, the remaining players can play on until they too are stripped, or simply, everyone can get in on the fun and take off their clothes!

What happens next is entirely up to the mood and disposition of the players.

When all is said and done, after the game, all clothing won or lost is sorted out, and players are returned their original table stake so that nobody walks away any poorer for the game.

Winning Strategy

As in other forms of poker, you should study your opponents to ascertain the best strategies to play - seeing who can be bluffed and who can't - and seeing whatever else there is to see!

Choose your opponents wisely - after all, win or lose, you want to have fun. If you have any memorable strip poker stories, write in and let us know!

MONEY MANAGEMENT

To be a winner at gambling, you must exercise sound money management principles and keep your emotions under control. The temptation to ride a winning streak too hard in the hopes of a big killing, or to bet wildly during a losing streak, trying for a quick comeback, can spell doom. Wins can turn into losses, and moderate losses can turn into a nightmare.

Instead, one must plan ahead and prepare for the game. And its important to understand the nature of the gamble.

In any gambling pursuit where luck plays a role, fluctuations in ones fortunes are common. It is the ability of the player to successfully deal with the ups and downs inherent in the gamble, that separate the smart gamblers from the losers.

Here are **the three important principles** of money management:

1. Never gamble with money you can't afford to lose - either financially or emotionally.

Do not gamble with needed funds no matter how "sure" any bet seems. The possibilities of losing are real, and if that loss will hurt, you're playing the fool.

2. Bankroll yourself properly.

Undercapitalization leaves a player vulnerable in two ways. First, a normal downward trend can wipe out a limited money supply. Second, and more important, the bettor may feel pressured by the shortage of capital and play less powerfully than smart play dictates.

If the amount staked on a bet is above your head, you're playing in the wrong game. Play only at levels of betting you feel comfortable with.

3. Know when to quit - set stop-loss limits.

What often separates the winners from the losers is that the winners, when winning, leave the table a winner, and when losing, restrict their losses to affordable amounts. Smart gamblers never allow themselves to get destroyed at the gamble.

Minimizing losses is the key. You can't always win. If you're losing, keep the losses affordable - take a break. You only want to play with a clear head.

When you're winning big, put a good chunk of these winnings in a "don't touch" pile, and play with the rest. You never want to hand all your winnings back to the casino. Should a losing streak occur, you're out of there - a winner!!!

GAMBLING CROSSWORD

Across

1. What they call Major League baseball. The ____.
5. Negative.
8. Initials of game Thorp made popular.
10. You lose this when you see no way to win.
11. Oriental game of skill.
12. No ____ off your back. Not with four aces.
14. The Spanish may yell these if they hit the jackpot.
15. Football and baseball star.
16. Initials of American game of skill.
17. What you did when all your money was lost.
21. The house advantage (spelled backwards).
22. This color rhymes with a popular card game.
26. Five in a row gives you this.
29. Winning low poker hand.
30. Baccarat betting spot.
31. Close.
32. These people have lots of money to gamble.
35. What every charity event has. A _____.

38. Clothing you wear.
40. When you always lose, you bowl a lot of these_____s.
41. The house profit.
45. You'll find these initials on a craps table.
47. A roulette bet.
48. State government gambling game.
49. Las Vegas is a city full of this.
50. What you need to legally gamble.

Down
1. The final act in poker.
2. Ace in the ____.
3. To begin betting.
4. Position in bridge.
5. Not yes.
8. Let me __.
9. Picture card.
11. You need a lot of this if you're wiped out..
12. You'll do a lot of this if you're wiped out.
13. Binion's downtown Las Vegas casino.
15. Famous playing cards brand.
18. You're this when you borrow gambling money and don't pay back. A____.
19. These professionals have lots of gambling money.
20. The gambler's ____. Money management curve.
23. Dishonest player. A ____.
24. Suit of love (singular).
25. Bets more money again in poker.
26. Sunny Southern Californian and Mexican spot to go after a win.
27. The last two letters of a plate wins can be saved.
28. Initials of giant appliance company (and Dickens novel).
33. First two letters of this tournament card game.
34. Lucky craps number.
35. A garbage card in poker.
36. Old saloon card game.
37. Didn't win. It happened yesterday.
38. Best hold 'em hand.
42. __ the money.
43. You get this way quickly after too many emotional losses.
44. __ is I, O' Lady Luck.
46. Spanish affirmative.

GAMBLING QUIZ

1. What is the main difference between a French roulette wheel and an American one?

_____

2. Who is the anchorman in blackjack?

_____

3. California poker games call this card a bug. What card are they referring to?

_____

4. What are the inside numbers in craps?

_____

5. All bets in American roulette give the casino a 5.26% edge with the exception of this bet, which gives the house a 7.89% edge. What bet is this?

_____

6. How many cards are there in a four deck shoe?

_____

7. You're dealt a pair of fives in blackjack. What is the correct play?

_____

8. How many possible combinations are there in two dice?

_____

9. What gambling game features the king number?

_____

10. When we talk about a carousel, what gambling game are we referring to?

_____

11. What is meant by paint in cards?

_____

12. Which position will win more often in baccarat, the Player or the Banker?

_____

13. What was the original slot machine? The Liberty Bell, the Mills High Top or the Watling Rol-A-Top?

_____

14. The snapper is a blackjack term referring to what?

_____

15. Cousins is a term used in what game?

_____

16. What is an oldsmobile in hold 'em poker?

_____

17. What is the best possible hand in video poker?

_____

18. What are the most numbers you can bet on in a straight keno ticket?

_____

19. What two hands in baccarat are called naturals?

_____

20. In blackjack, you're dealt two kings and the dealer shows a 6. What is the correct play?

_____

FIFTY-TWO
MAD, MAD GAMBLES

Introduction

The inventive and wacky ideas diehard gamblers come up with to satiate that unscratchable itch - to gamble on anything that moves or can be moved - helps make life interesting and exciting.

Cowpie bingo, betting on the way raindrops fall, insect racing, for just a few examples, are just drops in the bucket of countless ideas that may capture a gambler's imagination.

So, in this section, for some ideas on the lighter side of the coin, we present 52 mad, mad gambles, offbeat ways to pass time on an unusual wager you may not have thought of before.

Forget about that rainy day or long boring afternoon. Let's have some fun!

1. The Fly and the Cube

An old favorite needing but a wild fly and two sugar cubes for our first, mad, mad gambling game. Place two sugar cubes on a table and bet on the cube which will be landed on first by a fly.

2. Don't Touch

You're so irresistible, but, who can last longer, yourself or your friend, without touching one's own face. Not as easy as it sounds. You'll be amazed at all the itches you suddenly feel. Even more fun - make the wager on two complete strangers that can be observed unawares.

3. Food Obsession

Monitor two people in a discussion. The topic of food invariably comes up. Who will bring it up first?

4. "What?"

Again, two people are observed in a discussion. Bet on which conversant will say "what" more frequently in a five minute span. Get out the watches. Also good as an over and under wager.

5. Idiosynchrasies

Watch for a person's idiosyncrasies, whether it be a strange facial or body movement, or figure of speech. Each bettor picks a number for the amount of times he or she feels that movement will repeat in two minutes. The closest guess wins - an exact count gets credit for double.

6. Yes or No

Who can go longer without saying either "yes" or "no?" A fun bet with two people, a real bettor's heaven when betting on others.

7. A Day at the Races!

The classic "South of the Border" inspired bet. See if you can get hold of some Mexican jumping beans.

Make circles and place the beans within them. Bet on your hot tamale to escape the circle first.

8. At the Restaurant
Look over at the next table and choose an unsuspecting diner. Your partner chooses another. You're betting on your chosen diner to drink his or her drink before your opponent's does.

9. At the Restaurant - Over/Under
An over/under bet of the last wager. How many times will your star player lift their drink off the table. Closest number wins. An exact hit wins double.

10. License Plate Poker
Got a long drive and are bored in the car? Play license plate poker. Best five cards win. Can even play draw poker style. Discard some numbers, pick up more on the next plate. One can play the first white car, the other the first blue, or simply, the first cars you pass or that pass you.

11. Heads or Tails
Make it easy this time. Heads or tails?

12. The Big Bite
Lunacy can set in if you're a real gambling maniac. Bet on how many bites it will take someone to finish a sandwich.

13. Lots of Words
A long rainy day ahead? Go article by article in the newspaper and guess the number of words. Like I said, a long, rainy day. Bonus points for getting close.

14. The Penny Toss

In the big city we threw pennies against the wall. The closest penny to the wall is the winner. If you're a real killer at it, you may clean friends out of all their pennies.

15. The Ascetic Weight Watcher's Gamble.

A fast can be good to clean the body. Bet on who can go longer without eating dessert? Set a maximum limit if this exercise is pure torture. Warning, if you're serious about dropping pounds, don't bet cheesecakes.

16. The Serious Weight Watcher's Gamble.

You and your partner pick a diet and stick to it until the goal is reached. Should one go off the diet first, lots of bucks may be the penalty. Can also do cigarettes or other harmful habits as well.

17. Ice Cream Madness

Something for the real pigs. Get out the ice cream. I mean, how much can you really eat? You've got one hour baby. If you're a sadist; use beans!

18. Certified Crazies

Only for nuts and obsessed crazy's, see who can stand on one leg longer. It's not that easy, and its a barrel of laughs.

19. Drinks and Cigarettes

A barroom classic. Wet the edges of a glass and drape a napkin over it. Each player takes turns burning a hole in the napkin (within the lip) with a cigarette. The loser is the one who causes the napkin to finally collapse and also the one buying the next round.

20. What's Your Sign, Babe?
Want to make a nuisance out of yourself and meet people? Guess someone's astrological sign, then go and ask that person if you were right. Makes for a good bet as well.

21. Racing Insects
Get yourself some insects and race them. The critters can be found the world over.

22. Pumping Iron
Now we test ourselves for strength - and bet on it. Set up the field and see who can throw a kernel of popped popcorn farther. Try not to hit people twice your size.

23. Popcorn Basketball
Set up a glass in the middle of the table and it's best of five from the line.

24. Popcorn Football
Your opponent sets up a field goal target with his/her fingers - thumbs touch horizontally, and index fingers vertical. Three points for a field goal, six points if the shot goes in the mouth - touchdown!

25. Coin Football
With a quarter, you get three pushes using the back of your fingernails to get the coin hanging over the opposing edge of the table. Seven points for scoring in one push, six points for doing it in two, three points (field goal) for doing it in three. Off the table or after three pushes, the opponent takes possession.

26. Five Card War

Place five random cards face down on a table across from your opponent. Turn opposing cards up one at a time. Ace is high, deuce is low. Best of five cards determines the winner.

27. Dice Baseball

Get yourself a pair of dice. Each roll is a batter. 12 - home run, 11 - double, 10 - single, 8-9 - flyout, 7 - strikeout, 6 - groundout, runners advance one base, 4-5 - single, 3 - double play (leading runner out), 2 - (Roll again now. 2-7, sacrifice fly, 8-12, triple.) Three outs to an inning. Batter up!

28. Lucky 10, Unlucky 13

Turn over two cards. You get 1 point for each ten, jack, queen or king. All other cards are at face value. If two cards together add up to 13, the score doesn't count and you miss a turn. First to score *exactly* 21 wins. If more than 21 points are scored, back to zero you go.

29. The Napkin Drop

Drop a napkin from shoulder height and have it land within a circle marked off below. Two points for being wholly within the circle, one point for a partial. How good are you?

30. Spin and Walk

Spin a person seven times, and see if he or she can walk a straight line. Your turn now. It's not so easy to keep control, even with a bet at stake. If it's too easy or too hard, can spin more times or less.

31. Golf With a Little Spice

Golfers are no stranger to this concept. Every hole is worth another bet. If you're betting drinks, don't drive tonight or tomorrow. If you're betting money, concentrate on your game.

32. Paranoid in the City

In this mad, mad gamble, you compete against a friend in a crowded area. You must be very alert and quick for the first to get touched is *contaminated* and loses. A tough and wacky bet. The more crowded the situation, the greater the challenge. In a clothing store, if necessary, dive on a rack to avoid the "touch."

33. Rainmaker

How well can you predict the rain? Bet on the next day it will rain, or for rainy areas, what time it will begin, or how long the rain will last. Lots of fun when you're in the jungle.

34. In the Restaurant Again

Pit one diner against another. Of course, the unsuspecting diners have no knowledge you're betting on or against them. You're betting that the diner you're championing will hold onto his or her eating utensil longer than your opponent's. Once that spoon, fork or knife hits the table, the bet is over.

35. Still in the Restaurant

This time we want our player to get rid of the fork or spoon fast. (Opposite of #34.) Choose your franchise player wisely!

36. Watch Out for the Cement

How well can you spot a glued human? Better than your buddy? Two people are sitting in a park or other locale, though not together. Choose the player you feel will get up first. If the player you chose sat in cement, you may have to give odds.

37. The Annoyance Wager

Find a family member or friend who's reading and ask them if they want water. Ten seconds later, a mint? How about a cookie? What time is it? Keep going with questions until they blow up. How many disturbances will it take? An over and under wager.

38. Puffing Away

Bet on how many puffs of a cigarette a person will take before he or she puts out the flame.

39. The Classic Complainer

Some people complain at every meal. Can you guess how long it will take before the rumbling begins? Start the clock as soon as everyone is seated. Loser buys the meal.

40. The True Personality Test

As soon as someone leaves for the toilet, it's time to choose your wager. Will the toilet trotter come back smiling or with a straight face? (Ours is not to question why...)

41. Order of Consumption #1

You spot a likely couple at the next table. Which food will they taste first, the main dish, or a side order (such as the French Fries, vegetables etc.)?

42. Order of Consumption #2
Which dish will they finish first, the main one (sandwich, hamburger, fish etc.), or the side show?

43. Knowing Your Women
How well do you know the opposite sex, or your own? When a couple stands and prepares to walk, which side will the woman choose - or the man?

44. It's a Long Car Ride
Let's get bizarre and make a bet on the unsuspecting player's answer to this question. "What is the best thing that ever happened to you?" Can lead to an interesting discussion in any case.

45. Bet You on Dessert
See that full figured couple? Bet on whether they'll order dessert. You'll need to give odds though, say 4 to 1? The odds should be adjusted by size.

46. Skinny Chicken Week
Find a rail thin person. Will they go for desert? May want to make the odds 2 to 1?

47. The Neurotic Tester
Generally, when people pause to ponder a question, their eyes go either to the left or right as they think. Which way will they look?

48. Back to the Flies
Bet on the next fly that strays onto your table. Which way will it face? If you get really good at this, maybe you better start asking yourself some questions. If you learn how to train flies, you can make a good living

until opponents get wise.

49. The Return of the Fly

Bet on how many times a fly lands at your table within a five minute span. I don't know what your obsession is with flies, but in any case, an exact guess of the number wins double.

50. Sickness of the Mind Gamble

If your sense of humor is slightly distorted, this mad, mad gamble should appeal to you. Bet on how long it will take before someone either coughs, sneezes, wipes or blows their nose, burps, farts, yawns, clears their throat or hiccups.

51. Great Food!

At a large family or friendly meal. This is a fun wager and certainly a tough one to handicap when many diners are present. Wager on who will say the food is delicious first. Someone always does.

52. Send in Your Favorite Gamble!

We would love to hear from you. Send in your favorite gamble and in return, we'll send you a surprise!

WORLD CASINO GUIDE

Following is a complete guide to the cities and countries around the world which offer casino gambling!

Be aware that the games listed as being offered within a country may not be available at all its casinos, and sometimes, the addition of new games may not yet have found its way to our list.

In our world casino guide, we have only listed the more popular casino games as shown in our codes on the next page. All forms of baccarat such as Punto Banco, Chemin de Fer and others are simply listed under the generic title of baccarat in these listings.

We have made every attempt to be as accurate and complete as possible, but where we erred, please let us know so we can correct it for our readers in future editions.

CASINO INDEX

1- 26 or more casinos

2- 16-25 casinos

3- 6-15 casinos

4- 0-5 casinos

Europe

Austria - **3** B, BJ, P, R, SL.
Baden, Badgastein, Bregenz, Graz, Innsbruck, Kitzbuhel, Kleinwalsertal, Linz, Salzburg, Seefeld, Velden, Vienna.

Belgium - **3** B, BJ, R.
Blankenberg, Chaudfontaine, Dinant, Knokke, Middelkerke, Namur, Oostende

Bulgaria - **4** B, BJ, R, SL.
Sofia, Sunny Beach, Varna.

Canary Islands - **4** B, BJ, R, SL.
Maspalomas

Czech Republic - **3** BJ, R, SL.
Brno, Karlovy Vary, Kladno, Prague

Denmark - **4** B, BJ, R, SL.
Alborg, Arhus, Copenhagen, Odense, Vejle

Estonia - **4** BJ, R, SL.
Talinn

Finland - **2** BJ, R, SL, VP.

Hameenlinna, Helsinki, Imatra, Joensuu, Jyvaskyla, Kokkola, Kotka, Kuusamo, Kuusankoski, Lahti, Mariehamn, Mikkeli, Oulu, Pieksamaki, Savonlinna, Tampere, Tornio, Turku, Vaaksy, Vaasa.

France - **1** B, BJ, CR, R, SL.

Aix-en-Provence, Aix-les-Bains, Ajaccio, Allegre-les-Fumades, Amelie-les-Bains, Amneville, Antibes, Arcachon, Argeles-sur-Mer, Ax-les-Thermes, Bagneres-les-Bigorre, Bagnoles-de-L'Orne, Balaruc, Bandol, Benodet, Besancon, Biarritz, Bourbon-Lancy, Bourbone-les-Bains, Brides-les-Bains, Cabourg, Calais, Cannes, Cap Breton, Cap d' Agde, Carry-le-Rouet, Cassis-sur-Mer, Challes-les-Eaux, Chamonix, Cherbourg, Dax, Deauville, Dieppe, Dinard, Divonne-les-Bains, Dunkerque, Enghien-les-Bains, Evian-les-Bains, Font-Romeu, Forges-les-Eaux, Gerardmer, La Baule, La Grande-Motte, La Roche-Posay, Las Sables d'Olonne, Le Boulou, Luc-sur-Mer, Luxeuil les Bains, Lyon, Mandelieu Napoule, Megeve, Menton, Nice, Niederbronn-les-Bains, Palavas-les-Flots, Pau, Pornic, Pornichet, Royal Pontaillac, Saint-Amand-les-Eaux, Saint-Malo, Saint Raphael, Sainte Maxime, Santenay-les-Bains, Trouville, Vichy, Vittel.

Germany - **1** B, BJ, R, SL.

Aachen, Bad Bentheim, Bad Durkheim, Bad Ems, Bad Harzburg, Bad Homberg, Bad Kissingen, Bad Neuenahr, Bad Oeynhausen, Bad Prymont, Bad Reichenhall, Bad Wiessee, Bad Zwischenahn, Baden-Baden, Berlin, Bremen, Dortmund, Dresden, Garmisch-Partenkirchen, Hamburg, Hannover, Hittfeld, Homburg, Insel Borkum, Insel Norderney, Kassel, Konstanz, Leipzig, Lindau, Luebeck, Magdeburg, Mainz, Nennig/Mosel, Saarbrucken, Trier, Westerland, Wiesbaden.

Gibraltar - **4** B, BJ, CR, R, SL.

Gibraltor Town.

Greece - **4** B, BJ, R.
Athens, Corfu, Rhodes.

Hungary - **3** B, BJ, R, SL.
Budapest, Heviz, Sopron.

Italy - **4** B, BJ, CR, R
Campione D'Italia, St-Vincent, San Remo, Venice.

Latvia - **4** BJ, R, SL
Riga

Luxembourg - **4** BJ, R, SL.
Mondorf-les-Bains

Macedonia -**4** B, BJ, R, SL
Dojran, Gevgelija, Ohrid, Skopje

Malta - **4** B, BJ, CR, R.
St. Julian's/Sliema.

Moldova - **4** BJ, R, SL
Kishinev

Monaco -**4** B, BJ, CR, R, SL.
Monte Carlo.

Netherlands -**3** B, BJ, R, SL.
Amsterdam, Breda, Groningen, The Hague, Nijmegen, Rotterdam, Valkenburg, Zandvoort.

North Cyprus -**4** B, BJ, CR, R, SL.
Gazimagusa/Famagusta, Girne/Kyrenia, Lefkosa/Nicosia

Poland -**3** B, R, SL
Gdansk, Katowice, Krakow, Lodz, Poznan, Sopot, Szczecin, Warsaw, Wroclaw, Zakopane

Portugal - 3 B, BJ, CR, R, SL.
   Espinho, Estoril, Figueira da Foz, Madeira, Monte Gordo, Portimao, Pova de Varzim, Vilamoura

Romania - 4 B, BJ, R, SL.
   Bucharest

Russia - 3 B, BJ, CR, P, R, SL.
   Moscow, Sochi, St. Petersburg

Slovakia - 4 BJ, R, SL.
   Bratislava, Kosice, Zilina

Slovenia - 4 B, BJ, R, SL.
   Bled, Nova Gorica, Portoroz, Rogaska Slatina

Spain - 2 B, BJ, CR, R, SL.
   Barcelona, Benalmadena, Cadiz, La Coruna, Ibiza, Isla de la Toja, La Manga del Mar Menor, Lloret de Mar, Madrid, Marbella, Maspalomas (Grand Canary Island), Palma de Mallorca (Mallorca), Peralada, Puzol, San Sebastian, Santandar, Tenarife, Valladolid, Villa Joyosa, Zaragoza.

Sweden - 3 BJ, R.
   Gothenburg, Ljungby, Lysekil, Malmo, Ronneby, Skoevde, Stockholm, Sundsvall.

Switzerland -2
   Only Boule, a roulette-type game is offered.

Ukraine - 4 BJ, R.
   Kiev.

United Kingdom - 1 B, BJ, CR, R, SL.
   ENGLAND: Birkenhead, Birmingham, Blackpool, Bolton, Bournemouth, Bradford, Brighton, Bristol, Coventry, Derby, Groleston-on-Sea, Great Yarmouth, Hove, Huddersfield, Hull, Leeds, Leicester, Liverpool, London, Luton, Lytham St.

Annes, Manchester, Margate, Middlesborough, Newcastle-upon-Tyne, Northampton, Nottingham, Plymouth, Ramsgate, Reading, Salford, Scarborough, Sheffield, Southampton, Southend, Southport, Southsea, Stockport, Stoke-on-Trent, Sunderland, Torquay, Walsall, Wolverhampton.

ISLE OF MAN: Douglas.
ISLE OF WIGHT: Shanklin.
SCOTLAND: Aberdeen, Dundee, Edinburgh, Glasgow.
WALES: Cardiff, Swansea

Yugoslavia
Political instability leave casino industry in flux.

Africa

Benin -4
Cotonou.

Bophuthatswana -3 B, BJ, CR, R, SL.
Babelegi, Ga-Rankuwa, Mmabatho, Sun City, Taung Station, Thaba'nchu.

Botswana - 4 BJ, R, SL.
Gaborone.

Ciskei - 4 B, BJ, R, SL.
Bisho, Mdantsane

Comoros Islands -4 BJ, R, SL.
Moroni, Mitsamiouli.

Djibouti -4
Djibouti City.

Egypt - 3 B, BJ, R, SL.
Alexandria, Aswan, Cairo, Luxor.

Gabon - **4** BJ, R, SL.
Franceville, Libreville.

Gambia - **4** BJ, R, SL.
Banjul/Fajara Beach.

Ghana - **4** BJ, R, SL.
Accra, Kumasi, Tema.

Ivory Coast - **4** BJ, R, SL.
Abidjan.

Lesotho - **4** B, BJ, R, SL.
Maseru.

Liberia - **4** BJ, R, SL.
Monrovia.

Kenya - **3**. B, BJ, P, R, SL.
Kisumu, Mombasa, Nairobi.

Madagascar - **4**. BJ, R.
Antananarivo, Nosy-Be Island.

Mauritius - **3**. B, BJ, R, SL.
Belle Mare Beach, Curepipe, Flic-en-Flac Beach, Quatre Bornes, Port Louis, Rivere Noire, Triolet.

Morocco - **4**. B, BJ, CR, R, SL.
Marrakech, Mohammadia.

Nigeria - **3**. BJ, R, SL.
Abuja, Ibadan, Lagos, Port Harcourt.

Reunion - **4**.
Saint-Denis.

Senegal - **4**. BJ, R, SL
   Dakar.

Seychelles - **4**.
   Victoria.

Swaziland - **4**. B, BJ, R, SL.
   Ezulwini, Nhlangano, Piggs Peak.

Togo - **4**.
   Lome.

Transkei - **4**. B, BJ,R, SL.
   Wild Coast.

Tunisia - **4**.
   Djerba Island, Tunis.

Venda - **4**. B, BJ, R, SL.
   Thohoyandou.

Zaire - **4**. BJ, R, SL.
   Kinshasha.

Zambia - **4**. BJ, R, SL.
   Lusaka, Ndola.

Zimbabwe -**4** B, BJ, R, SL.
   Juliasdale, Kariba, Victoria Falls.

Asia

Macau - **3** B, BJ, CR, K, R, SL.
   Macau, Taipa Island.

Malaysia - **4** B, BJ, K, R, SL.
   Genting Highlands.

Nepal - **4** B, BJ, P, R, SL.
   Kathmandu.

Philippines - **3** B, BJ, CR, K, R, SL.
   Angeles City, Bacolod City, Cauayan, Cebu City, Davao City, Manila, Olongapo City, Tagaytay City.

South Korea - **3** B, BJ, CR, P, R, SL -
   Cheju-Do, Inch'on City, Kyonju, Mt. Sorak, Pusan, Seoul, Songni-San Park, Taejon.

Sri Lanka - **4** BJ, R.

Turkey - **1** B, BJ, P, R, SL.
   Adana, Akbuk, Alanya, Ankara, Antalya, Atakoy, Ayvalik, Bodrum, Bursa, Cesme, Istanbul, Izmir, Kemer, Kusadasi, Marmaris, Mersin, Nevsehir, Pamukkale, Side, Silivri.

Australia/South Pacific

Australia - **3** B, BJ, CR, K, P. R, SL.
   Adelaide, Alice Springs, Broadbeach, Canberra, Darwin, Hobart (Tasmania), Launceston, Perth, Townsville.

New Caledonia -**4** B, BJ, R, SL.
   Noumea.

New Zealand -**4**
   Auckland, Christchurch.

Vanuatu -**4** B, BJ, R, SL.
   Noumea.

Central/South America

Argentina - **2** B, BJ, CR, R, SL.
Alta Gracia, Colon, Comodoro Rivadavia, Gualeguaychu, Puerto Iguazu, La Cumbre, La Rioja, Mar del Plata, Mendoza, Miramar, Necochea, Parana, Pinamar, Puerto Madryn, Resistencia, Rosario de a Frontera, Salta, San Carlos de Bariloche, San Miguel de los Andes, San Miguel de Tucuman, Termas de Rio Hondo, Vall de Las Lenas.

Bolivia -**4** BJ, R, SL.
Cochabamba, La Paz, Santa Cruz

Chile -**3** B, BJ, R.
Arica, Coquimbo, Iquique, Pucon, Puerto Varas, Vina del Mar.

Columbia - **2** BJ, CR, P, R, SL
Barranquilla, Bogota, Cali, Cartagena, Girardot, Medellin, San Andres Island, Santa Marta

Costa Rica - **3** BJ, CR, P, R, SL.
Puntarenas, Quepos, San Jose.

Ecuador - **2** BJ, CR, R, SL.
Ambato, Cuenca, Guayaquil, Machala, Quito, Punta Carnero, Quito, Salinas, Santo Domingo de los Colorados, Tena, Tulcan.

Honduras - **4** B, BJ, P, R, SL.
San Pedro Sula, Tegucigalpa

Panama - **3** BJ, CR, P, R, SL.
Chiriqui Highlands, Colon, Panama City.

Paraguay - **3** B, BJ R, SL.
Asuncion, Ciudad Del Este, Pedro Juan Caballero, San Bernardino.

Peru - **4** BJ, R, SL.
Lima

Suriname -**4** BJ, R, SL.
Paramaribo.

Uruguay - **2** B, BJ, R, SL.
Atlantida, Carmelo, Chuy, Colonia, Colonia del Sacramento, Fray Bentos, La Coronilla, La Paloma, Montevideo, Paysundu, Piriapolis, Punta del Este, Rivera.

Bahamas/Caribbean

Antigua -**3** BJ, CR, R SL.
Dickenson Bay, Deep Bay, St John's, Mamora Bay.

Aruba - **3** B, BJ, CR, P, R, SL.
Oranjestad.

Bahamas - **4** B, BJ, CR, R, SL, VP
Freeport, Lacaya, Nassau.

Bonaire - **4**. B, BJ, CR, R, SL.
Kralendijk.

Curacao - **3** BJ, CR, P, R, SL.
Willemstad.

Dominican Republic - **3** B, BJ, CR, R, SL.
Puerto Plata, Punta Cana, San Pedro de Macoris, Santo Domingo.

Guadeloupe - **4** B, BJ, CR, R.
Gosier, Saint-Francois.

Haiti - **4** BJ, CR, R, SL.
  Petionville, Port-au-Prince.

Martinique - **4** B, BJ, CR, R.
  Fort-de France, Schoelcher.

Puerto Rico - **3** B, BJ, CR, R, SL.
  Dorado Beach, Humacao, Las Croabas, Mayaguez, Ponce, San Juan, Santurce.

St. Kitts - **4** B, BJ, CR, P, R, SL.
  Basseterre.

St. Maarten - **3** B, BJ, CR, R, SL.
  Philipsburg.

St. Vincent -**4** BJ, R, SL.
  Kingstown.

Turks and Caicos - **4** BJ, SL, R
  Providenciales

North America

CANADA CASINO GUIDE

As in the United States, gambling is proliferating in Canada Casinos have opened in provinces from the Yukon Territory to Quebec with more than 25 casinos in operation.

Alberta - Calgary, Edmonton, Fort McMurray, Grand Prairie, Lethbridge, Medicine Hat, St. Albert.

British Columbia - Burnaby, Mission, Nanaimo, Prince George, Quesnel, Richmond, Surrey, Vancouver, Victoria, Westbank.

Manitoba - Winnipeg.

Ontario - Ottawa, Windsor.

Quebec - Montreal.

Saskatchewan - Kenosee Lake, Lloydminister, Melville, Moose Jaw, North Battleford, Prince ALbert, Regina, Saskatoon, Swift Current, Yorkton.

Yukon - Dawson City.

UNITED STATES CASINO GUIDE

Following is a state by state listing of legalized casino gambling.

Arizona - Indian reservation gambling.

California - There are close to 500 clubs licensed for poker with the highest concentration of poker club located in Gardena, a Los Angeles suburb. Indian reservation gambling is scattered around the state as well.

Colorado - Small stakes gambling legalized in Cripple Creek, Black Hawk, and Central City. Also Indian reservation gambling at Ute reservations in Southwest Colorado.

Connecticut - Indian reservation gambling at North America's most profitable casino at Foxwood.

Florida - Indian reservation gambling.

Illinois - Riverboat gambling.

Iowa - Riverboat and Indian reservation gambling.

Louisiana - Riverboat gambling and Indian reservation gambling. Also, gambling has arrived in New Orleans.

Michigan - Indian gambling on more than 15 reservations.

Minnesota - Indian reservation gambling.

Mississippi - More than two dozen riverboats throughout the state, mostly centered in Biloxi, Tunica, and Gulfport.

Missouri - Riverboat gambling.

Montana - Indian reservation gambling.

Nevada - The home of the world's gambling capital, Las Vegas. Also, Laughlin (near Arizona border), Reno - *the Biggest Little City in the World*, Lake Tahoe (near California border), and more than 50 small towns and cities around the state.

New Jersey - Home of 12 Atlantic City casinos, the East Coast's attempted counterpart to Las Vegas.

New York - Indian reservation gambling.

North Dakota - Indian reservation and small stake gambling in more than two dozen locales.

Oregon - Indian reservation gambling.

South Dakota - More than 50 small casinos in Deadwood, and various Indian reservation gambling scattered around the state as well.

Wisconsin - Indian reservation gambling.

Las Vegas Casino/Hotel Numbers

(The 2nd number listed is the local phone - 702 area code)

Aladdin	(1-800-634-3424)	736-0111
Anthony's	(1-800-634-6617)	733-7777
Arizona Charlie's	(1-800-342-2695)	258-5200
Bally's	(1-800-634-3434)	739-4111
Barbary Coast	(1-800-634-6755)	737-7111
Barcelona	(1-800-223-6330)	644-6300
Best Western	(1-800-634-6501)	731-2020
Boardwalk	(1-800-635-4581)	735-2400
Boulder Station	(1-800-683-7777)	367-2411
Bourbon Street	(1-800-634-6956)	737-7200
Caesars Palace	(1-800-634-6661)	731-7110
California Hotel	(1-800-634-6255)	385-1222
Casino Royale	(1-800-854-7666)	737-3500
Circus Circus	(1-800-634-3450)	734-0410
Continental Hotel	(1-800-634-6641)	737-5555
Days Inn	(1-800-325-2344)	388-1400
Days Inn-Town	(1-800-634-6541)	731-2111
Debbie Reynolds	(1-800-633-1777)	734-0711
Desert Inn	(1-800-634-6906)	733-4444
El Cortez	(1-800-634-6703)	385-5200
Excalibur	(1-800-937-7777)	597-7777
Fitzgeralds	(1-800-274-LUCK)	388-2400
Flamingo Hilton	(1-800-HILTONS)	733-3111
Four Queens	(1-800-634-6045)	385-4011
Fremont	(1-800-634-6182)	385-3232
Frontier Hotel	(1-800-421-7806)	794-8200
Gold Coast	(1-800-331-5334)	367-7111
Golden Nugget	(1-800-634-3403)	385-7111
Gold Spike	(1-800-634-6703)	384-8444
Hacienda Hotel	(1-800-634-6713)	739-8911
Harrah's	(1-800-HARRAHS)	369-5000
Holiday Casino	(1-800-635-4581)	735-2400
Horseshoe	(1-800-622-6468)	382-1600
Hotel Continental	(1-800-634-6641)	737-5555
Hotel San Reno	(1-800-522-7366)	739-9000

Howard Johnson	(1-800-654-2000) 798-1111
Imperial Palace	(1-800-634-6441) 731-3311
Jackie Gaughan's	(1-800-634-6575) 386-2110
King 8	(1-800-634-3488) 736-8988
Lady Luck	(1-800-Lady-Luck) 477-3000
Las Vegas Club	(1-800-634-6532) 385-1664
Las Vegas Hilton	(1-800-HILTONS) 732-5111
Luxor	(1-800-288-1000) 262-4000
MGM Grand Hotel	(1-800-929-1111) 891-1111
Maxim Hotel	(1-800-634-6987) 731-4300
Mirage	(1-800-627-6667) 791-7111
Nevada Hotel	(1-800-637-5777) 385-7311
Palace Station	(1-800-544-2411) 367-2411
Quality Inn	(1-800-634-6617) 733-7777
Rainbow Vegas	(1-800-634-6635) 386-6166
Rio Suite Casino	(1-800-888-1808) 252-7777
Riviera Hotel	(1-800-634-3420) 734-5110
Royal Hotel	(1-800-634-6118) 735-6117
Sahara Hotel	(1-800-634-6666) 737-2111
Sam's Town	(1-800-634-6371) 456-7777
Sands Hotel	(1-800-634-6901) 733-5000
Santa Fe Hotel	(1-800-872-6823) 658-4900
Sheraton Desert Inn	(1-800-634-6906) 733-4444
Showboat Hotel	(1-800-826-2800) 385-9123
Silver City	732-4152
Stardust Hotel	(1-800-824-6033) 732-6111
Treasure Island	(1-800-944-7444) 894-7111
Tropicana	(1-800-634-4000) 739-2222
Union Plaza	(1-800-634-6575) 386-2110
Vacation Village	(1-800-658-5000) 897-1700
Vegas World	(1-800-634-6277) 382-2000
Westward Ho	(1-800-634-6803) 731-2900
Western Hotel	(1-800-634-6703) 384-8420
Whiskey Pete's	(1-800-367-7383) 382-1212

Atlantic City Casino/Hotel Numbers

(The 2nd number listed is the local phone - 609 area code)

Bally's Park Place	(1-800-772-7777)	340-2000
Caesars	(1-800-443-0104)	348-4411
Claridge	(1-800-257-5277)	340-3400
Grand (Bally's)	(1-800-257-8677)	347-7111
Harrah's Casino	(1-800-2- HARRAH)	441-5000
Merv Griffin Resorts Int'l	(1-800-336-MERV)	344-6000
Sands	(1-800-446-4678)	733-5000
Showboat	(1-800-621-0200)	343-4000
TropWorld	(1-800-THE-TROP)	340-4000
Trump's Castle	(1-800-441-5551)	441-2000
Trump Plaza	(1-800-677-7378)	441-6000
Trump Taj Majal	(1-800-825-8786)	449-1000

Laughlin Casino/Hotel Numbers

(The 2nd number listed is the local phone - 702 area code)

Colorado Bell	(1-800-458-9500)	298-4000
Edgewater Hotel	(1-800-67-RIVER)	298-2453
Flamingo Hilton	(1-800-FLAMINGO)	298-5111
Golden Nugget	(1-800-955-SLOT)	298-7111
Harrah's Casino	(1-800-HARRAHS)	298-4600
Pioneer Hotel	(1-800-634-3469)	298-2442
Ramada Express	1-800-343-4533)	298-4200
Regency Casino		298-2439
Riverside Resort	(1-800-227-3849)	298-2535
Sam's Town Gold River	(1-800-835-7904)	298-2242

ANSWERS TO PUZZLES

Answers to Crossword

```
S H O W       N O       B J
H O P E   G O     S W E A T
O L E S   R   B O       C H
W E N T H O M E B R O K E
D       E G D E     U     H
O C H R E   S   B I N G O
W H E E L       B A N K E R
N E A R       J       S
A R A B S   R A F F L E
A T T I R E   A   A   O S
C   S   V I G O R I S H
E S   E V E N   L O T T O
S I N S   N   I D       E
```

Answers to Gambling Quiz

1. French wheel has one only zero, the American 0 and 00.
2. The anchorman plays to the dealer's right at "third base."
3. The joker.
4. 5, 6, 8 and 9.
5. The five # bet.
6. 208.
7. Double down.
8. 36.
9. Keno.
10. Slots.
11. The jack, queen and king.
12. Banker.
13. Liberty Bell.
14. Blackjack.
15. Roulette.
16. 9, 8.
17. Royal Flush
18. 15.
19. 8 and 9.
20. Stand

THE GAMBLER'S LOGBOOK

Date	Game Played	W	L	$ Bet	Time	Average

THE GAMBLER'S LOGBOOK

Date	Game Played	W	L	$ Bet	Time	Average

120

Baccarat Master Card Counter
NEW WINNING STRATEGY!

For the **first time**, Gambling Research Institute releases the **latest winning techniques** at baccarat. This **exciting** strategy, played by big money players in Monte Carlo and other exclusive locations, is based on principles that have made insiders and pros **hundreds of thousands of dollars** counting cards at blackjack - card counting!

NEW WINNING APPROACH

This brand **new** strategy now applies card counting to baccarat to give you a **new winning approach,** and is designed so that any player, with just a little effort, can successfully take on the casinos at their own game - and win!

SIMPLE TO USE, EASY TO MASTER

You learn how to count cards for baccarat without the mental effort needed for blackjack! No need to memorize numbers - keep the count on the scorepad. Easy-to-use, play the strategy while enjoying the game!

LEARN WHEN TO BET BANKER, WHEN TO BET PLAYER

No longer will you make bets on hunches and guesses - use the GRI Baccarat Master Card Counter to determine when to bet Player and when to bet Banker. You learn the basic counts (running and true), deck favorability, when to increase bets and much more in this **winning strategy**.

LEARN TO WIN IN JUST ONE SITTING

That's right! After **just one sitting** you'll be able to successfully learn this powerhouse strategy and use it to your advantage at the baccarat table. Be the best baccarat player at the table - the one playing the odds to **win**! Baccarat can be beaten. The Master Card Counter shows you how!

FREE BONUS!

Order now to receive **absolutely free**, The Basics of Winning Baccarat. One quick reading with this great primer shows you how to play and win.

To order, send $50 by bank check or money order to:

Cardoza Publishing.P.O. Box 1500, Cooper Station, New York, NY 10276

Pro-Master II Lotto/Lottery Strategies

Prof Jones' Ultimate Winning Strategy for Non-Computer Users

Finally, after years of research into winning lotto tickets, Prof Jones has developed the ultimate in **winning jackpot strategies** for non-computer users! This **new powerhouse** gives you the **latest** in winning lotto strategies!

EASY TO USE - MINUTES A DAY TO WINNING JACKPOTS!

These **scientific winning systems** can be used successfully by anyone! Spend only **several minutes a day** inputting past winning numbers into the master templates and this **amazing system** quickly and **scientifically** generates the numbers that have the **best chances** of making you rich.

THE MASTER LOTTO/LOTTERY STRATEGIES AND MORE!

All the goodies of the Master Lotto/Lottery strategies - the winning systems, instruction guides, clear working template and bonus templates - are included in this **powerful winning strategy**, plus such **extra** features as the 3-Ball, 4-Ball and 6-Ball Sum Total charts. You also receive...

100 WHEELING SYSTEMS

That's right, **100** advanced Dimitrov Wheeling Systems - **double** the systems of the excellent Master Lotto/Lottery package! You'll be using the **most powerful** lotto and lottery winning systems ever designed.

BONUS

Free with this **super strategy** are 15 Positional Analysis templates, 10 each 3-Ball, 4-Ball, 6-Ball Sum Total Templates & 15 Best Number templates!

EXTRA BONUS

Order now and you'll receive, **absolutely free** with your order, the extra bonus, 7 Insider Winning Tips - a conside guide to **extra winning strategies**!

$50.00 Off! This $99.95 strategy is now only $49.95 with this coupon!

FOUR FUN HANDHELD CASINO GAMES!

These **exciting palm-sized** games made by Saitek, *the world leader in intelligent electronic games* can be taken anywhere! They feature **superb sound effects** and **large LCD screens** to bring you the excitement and challenge of Las Vegas casino play!

SAITEK PRO BLACKJACK - $59.95

LAS VEGAS EXCITEMENT/LEARN TO WIN MONEY - Have fun and learn how to win at the same time with this great blackjack computer. This exciting device allows you to improve your skills so when you hit the real casino, you're prepared to be a winner. All the features of casino blackjack are included along with exciting options.
PACKED WITH FEATURES - Choose any casino environment you want. Play against 1-6 deck games; choose any number of players at the table, one to four. You won't lose your shirt - bets between $10 and $1,000 are allowed. The built-in coach gives advice on all the options: hitting, standing, splitting, doubling down and insurance; and even introduces you to winning card counting methods!

SAITEK PRO VIDEO POKER - $59.95

Another fun and exciting winner from Saitek, this fast-paced, action-packed and easy-to-play game is difficult to put down. Play once and you're hooked forever!
TWO CHALLENGING GAMES IN ONE - Test your skills against *Jacks or Better* Video Poker and *Deuces Wild*. **Random shuffling** keeps play **realistic** - just like in the casinos. Bet from one coin to five and **play to win**. Go for the Royal Flush jackpot!
EXTRA FEATURES - Hold-Call buttons; **Increase Bet** button for aggressive play; **Credit Button**, plus shows payoffs and probabilities for **every** winning hand. Want to know the best play? Click **Hint Button**, and the on-screen tutor provides **best play**.

SAITEK PRO POKER - $59.95

REALISTIC POKER CHALLENGE - Imagine, take your Friday night poker game with you! You bet, call, raise, fold and even bluff just as in real poker. But be careful, Cautious Clay, Mustang Mel and Dr. Wynne - the three real-life poker characters **built into the game** - play to win also. There's the cool, statistical player, the aggressive, bullying player and the cautious, conservative player.
IMPROVE YOUR GAME - Test your skills against each opponents strategies and styles; the press of a button changes the players seats to keep you on your toes.
Extra features such as *Hold-Call*, *Options*, *Hint* and *Credit Buttons* keep game realistic. *On-screen tutor* provides tips on better strategy.

also...SAITEK ROULETTE - $59.95

PROFESSIONAL VIDEO POKER STRATEGY
Win at Video Poker - With the Odds!

At last, for the **first time,** and for **serious players only,** the GRI **Professional Video Poker** strategy is released so you too can play to win! **You read it right** - this strategy gives you the **mathematical advantage** over the casino and what's more, it's **easy to learn!**

PROFESSIONAL STRATEGY SHOWS YOU HOW TO WIN WITH THE ODDS
This **powerhouse strategy,** played for **big profits** by an **exclusive** circle of **professionals,** people who make their living at the machines, is now made available to you! You too can win - with the odds - and this **winning strategy** shows you how!

HOW TO PLAY FOR A PROFIT
You'll learn the **key factors** to play on a **pro level:** which machines will turn you a profit, break-even and win rates, hands per hour and average win per hour charts, time value, team play and more! You'll also learn big play strategy, alternate jackpot play, high and low jackpot play and key strategies to follow.

WINNING STRATEGIES FOR ALL MACHINES
This **comprehensive, advanced pro package** not only shows you how to win money at the 8-5 progressives, but also, the **winning strategies** for 10s or better, deuces wild, joker's wild, flat-top, progressive and special options features.

BE A WINNER IN JUST ONE DAY
In just one day, after learning our strategy, you will have the skills to **consistently win money** at video poker - with the odds. The strategies are easy to use under practical casino conditions.

BONUS - PROFESSIONAL PROFIT EXPECTANCY FORMULA ($15 VALUE)
For serious players, we're including this bonus essay which discusses the profit expectancy principles of video poker and how to relate them to real dollars and cents in your game.

To order, send $50 by check or money order to <u>Cardoza Publishing</u>

THE CARDOZA CRAPS MASTER
Three Big Strategies!
Exclusive Offer! - Not Available Anywhere Else

Here It is! **At last**, the **secrets** of the **Grande-Gold Power Sweep**, **Molliere's Monte Carlo Turnaround** and the **Montarde-D'Girard Double Reverse** - three big strategies - are made available and presented for the **first time anywhere**! These powerful strategies are designed for the serious craps player, one wishing to bring the best odds and strategies to hot tables, cold tables and choppy tables.

1. The Grande-Gold Power Sweep (Hot Table Strategy)

This **dynamic strategy** takes maximum advantage of hot tables and shows the player methods of amassing small **fortunes quickly** when numbers are being thrown fast and furious. The Grande-Gold stresses aggressive betting on wagers the house has no edge on! This previously unreleased strategy will make you a powerhouse at a hot table.

2. Molliere's Monte Carlo Turnaround (Cold Table Strategy)

For the player who likes betting against the dice, **Molliere's Monte Carlo** Turnaround shows how to turn a cold table into hot cash. Favored by an exclusive circle of professionals who will play nothing else, the uniqueness of this strongman strategy is that the vast majority of bets **give absolutely nothing away to the casino**!

3. The Montarde-D'Girard Double Reverse (Choppy Table Strategy)

This **new** strategy is the **latest** and **most exciting development** in recent years. **Learn how** to play the optimum strategies against the tables when the dice run hot and cold (a choppy table) with no apparent reason. **The Montarde-d'Girard Double Reverse** shows you how you can **generate big profits** while less knowledgeable players are ground out by choppy dice. And, of course, the majority of our bets give nothing away to the casino!

BONUS!!! - Order now, and receive **The Craps Master-Professional Money Management Formula** ($15 value) **absolutely free**! Necessary for serious players and **used by the pros**, it features the unique stop-loss ladder To order send ~~$75~~ $50 by check or money order to: <u>Cardoza Publishing,</u>

126

127